RELEASE YOUR
WOW!

RELEASE YOUR
WOW!

7 Steps to Self-Awareness
and Personal Fulfilment

Rennie Gould

urbanepublications.com

First published in Great Britain in 2016 by Urbane Publications Ltd
Suite 3, Brown Europe House, Gleaming Wood Drive, Chatham, Kent ME5 8RZ
Copyright ©Rennie Gould, 2016

A CIP catalogue record for this book is available from the British Library.

ISBN 978-1-909273-55-9
EPUB 978-1-909273-56-6
KINDLE 978-1-909273-57-3

Design and Typeset by Julie Martin
Cover by Julie Martin

urbanepublications.com

MIX
Paper from
responsible sources
FSC® C013604

The publisher supports the Forest Stewardship Council® (FSC®), the leading international forest-certification
organisation. This book is made from acid-free paper from an FSC®-certified provider. FSC is the only
forest-certification scheme supported by the leading environmental organisations, including Greenpeace.

for Canberra William Gould & Elsie Gould

CONTENTS

Introduction

What this book is designed to do

Quite simply this book is to help you achieve *Self-Awareness* and *Personal Fulfilment* by helping you become the person you should be and to express this true self in all areas of your life. It will also encourage you to push your *Authenticity* to its limits to pursue your *Life Goals* and *Life Purpose*.

This book reflects the latest theories behind *Mindfulness, Neuroscience, Epigenetics* and *Positive Psychology* and weaves them into an integrated framework to create both insight and practical guidance. This book therefore has some important things to say about who you are and what you should be doing with your life.

How this book came about

For about ten years I had been reviewing the latest discoveries in science to see if I could benefit from them. In particular, I was looking to become more calm and less tense, to be more fully engaged in life's experiences, to identify my particular strengths and essential values and to develop the confidence to fully express them in all areas of life. I came to realise that although mindfulness, neuroscience, epigenetics and positive psychology were important in their own right, they could make a much more powerful contribution if they could be linked together in some way to exploit their collective value.

I therefore decided to try and bring them together in a meaningful way and this task ultimately took over from everything else I was doing. However, for a long time I was merely juggling these concepts around in my head and wondering what to do with them, until slowly but surely a logical framework took shape and the *7-Steps* were born. As I then began to share my understanding and framework with whoever would listen, I realised that my own issues were common to many people and became convinced that everyone should share in the many valuable insights coming from the sciences and elsewhere and therefore *Release Your WOW!* was born.

If you are looking to achieve your full potential, I am confident you will find this book both interesting and useful. Actually, I hope I am under-shooting here because I want it to be much more than that - I want it to be *transformational.*

My objectives in writing this book

To explore what science (and sometimes non-science) can tell us about our capabilities

To integrate these insights into a progressive framework to allow everyone to achieve self-awareness and personal fulfilment

To produce an insightful, entertaining and inspiring book

This is also something of the personal story of my own search for authenticity and for its ultimate expression which ironically has led to the writing of this book.

The themes and concepts presented support the more rational and humanistic view of life that assumes our essential self comes from within rather than from without and in the absence of any divine entity to direct our lives, we must find our own individual sense of purpose and meaning. Although the transformational power of belief and faith is fully understood, for those of us without religious faith, this power must come from a belief in our unique capabilities and from our ability to determine our own destiny.

But in the final analysis, I don't think it really matters where we are coming from as the framework and insights contained in this book can help all of us, irrespective of our belief system, to become the person we are supposed to be and to celebrate this fact.

About Me

In my day job, I work with individuals and groups to help them become more effective in pursuing personal and organisational goals and have trained many hundreds of people in scores of organisations around the world. I have a Master's Degree specialising in strategy and organisational behaviour and have published a book based on this experience and taught at universities in the UK. I therefore usually describe myself as a semi-academic, with one foot in the world of academic theory and the other in the world of practical implementation. This might seem an unlikely balancing act but I believe my skills in seeking out new ideas and in helping people utilise them in the real world, provides me with the ideal background for the task I have taken on with this book.

My consultancy philosophy has never been one of *telling* but one of *sharing* – to introduce elements of my experience and knowledge in a way that allows for personal implementation. I'm sure this is the right way to go and I continue to use this philosophy throughout this book. I don't believe it is my place to give you advice, but to introduce you to ideas and concepts that I have found useful and believe you will too. In a world where everybody seems to have their own personal trainer, perhaps you can just see me as your own personal consultant - someone who has done the hard work of gathering together all the necessary insights into a practical framework for you to use whenever you like.

The 7-Step Framework

I believe the latest insights from the various branches of science can now be brought together to create a *formula* for achieving self-awareness and personal fulfilment:

(Awareness ✦ *Authenticity* ✦ *Well-Being* ✦ *Expression* ✦
Fulfilment ✦ *Gratitude)*
= *Self-Awareness* + *Personal Fulfilment*

All these elements are valuable in their own right and can deliver significant personal value, but when linked together as part of an integrated framework, their contribution in achieving self-awareness and personal fulfilment is transformed. These elements therefore form the structure of the book, together with a further element, *Insight*, which provides the essential, early understanding to fully exploit each step.

Release Your WOW! takes the view that many common problems, many of which can be traced back to a lack of confidence and self-esteem, will fade into the background if we are better able to focus our energy on *being* the person we were always supposed to be and to celebrate this fact.

Release Your WOW!

7 Steps to Self-Awareness & Personal Fulfilment

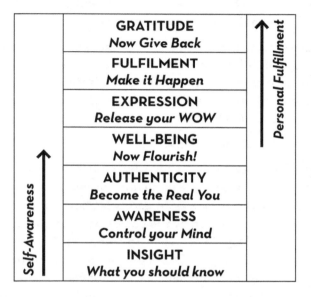

The *7-Steps* are a logical progression that builds understanding and the confidence to make the changes we might want to make to ourselves and our situation. Each step is designed to introduce the appropriate ideas and techniques just when you need them and to guide you through mindfulness, neuroscience, genetics and positive psychology (with a little bit of NLP and CBT thrown in for good measure) to ensure we extract the essence of what these disciplines have to offer.

Each chapter will give you all the understanding and insights necessary to make the best use of each step in the process towards *Self-Awareness and Personal Fulfilment* to become your true self. I firmly believe that if you know *how* something works, you will be more inclined to believe it *will* work and therefore more inclined to *make* it work, particularly as having the right beliefs and expectations are fundamental in making any change.

There is some repetition and reiteration of the key points throughout this book and this is deliberate as I have found in my own reading that sometimes a slightly different explanation can make all the difference in helping the penny to suddenly drop.

Description of the 7 Steps

The 7-Steps start with *Insight* which relates the latest finding in science to give us an understanding of how the brain and mind works. In particular, how our brain becomes programmed by the combination of our *Genetic Blueprint* and *Life Experiences* to create our *Current Self* with our *Emerged Characteristics* and *Beliefs and Expectations* that automatically programme all of our *Thoughts, Feelings, Behaviour and Body Processes*. This understanding is essential for making any subsequent changes to ourselves and to our situation.

Then in *Awareness*, we learn how to turn away from those negative thoughts and feelings to escape the chatter and noise that often distract our attention, but instead to learn how to control our mind, to fully engage with the present moment and to become mindful of all our positive experiences. Ultimately it will be this ability to focus our attention at will that will allow us to re-programme our brain and to change our situation.

In *Authenticity* we learn the value of *Acceptance* and

discover our *Key Attributes, Essential Values, Motivations and Aspirations* that constitute our *Authentic Self* and learn how to use *Affirmations* and *Visualizations* to create a *New Positive Self-image* that encapsulates every aspect of our *Authentic Self* which then fully engages with the present moment.

In *Well-Being*, we will utilise the findings of positive psychology to create an enhanced sense of well-being and self-worth by exploiting our *Authentic Self* in our main areas of life, thereby putting our *Authentic Energy-in-Motion* and giving our lives a greater sense of purpose and meaning.

Additionally, we will create the essential supportive infrastructure of positive emotions, memories, activities and relationships to provide heightened levels of confidence, optimism and resilience that will allow us to *Flourish*.

In *Expression* we push our authenticity and the increasing confidence that comes from being our real selves to its fullest extent to release our *WOWS!* that creates the inner energy and excitement that is essential to propel us towards our *Life Goals* and *Life Purpose*.

In *Fulfilment*, our *WOW Energy-in-Motion* goes out into the world to create the circumstances and opportunities that will appear as part of our journey towards our *Life Goals* and *Life Purpose* which will act like stars on the horizon to keep us on track and moving in the right direction.

Finally in *Gratitude*, we learn to give thanks for our own fulfilment but more importantly we will utilise those key attributes and insights gained from our own journey of personal fulfilment to *Give Back* and to help others find their own way.

Release Your WOW! is about becoming the person you were meant to be if only you knew how. It takes you on a journey of discovery that introduces all the main elements of change in the right order and at the right time to build the confidence in your own ability to make the changes you need to make to achieve *Self-awareness* and *Personal Fulfilment*.

How to Use the Book

There is a *Self-Diagnostic Questionnaire* in the Appendix that can be used to provide you with an understanding of where you currently are in your own journey towards *Self-awareness and Personal Fulfilment* to help you to identify those areas where you might devote your initial attention, although it might be useful to strengthen most of the areas over time and to keep them under review.

Although the steps are written to create a logical progression, you might well find that your own issues do not follow this logic and you could for example identify you are relatively strong in the later steps but have issues lower down. This is most people's experience, even my own, where I am strong on *Gratitude*, but still have issues in *Awareness*.

You should therefore not be concerned if you need to move around the steps in a random order as there is no right order, only your right order, nor is there a set amount of time you should devote to the exercises as this depends upon your area of focus and how much work you believe you need to do. In fact, my hope is that this book is not just a one-off read, but is something you can keep coming back to whenever you need to re-affirm your belief in who you are and what you are doing or whenever those negative thoughts and feelings need putting back into their rightful place.

Quotes

Throughout the book, you will also find quotes from a variety of science-based authors whose work has been fundamental to the development of the 7 Steps, together with quotes from those from the more spiritual side of the fence whose gift for explanation and communication enhance our understanding and inspire us to action.

There are also quotes from those who have already used the self-diagnostic questionnaire as the starting point for their own journey towards self-awareness and personal fulfilment, together with observations drawn from my own experience that will hopefully give you further insights.

Review Questions & Exercises

There are also review questions at the end of each step to help you reflect on your own situation and to prepare you for the exercises that follow. These well-proven exercises are mainly drawn from Mindfulness, Positive Psychology, Cognitive Behaviour Therapy (CBT) and Neuro-Linguistic Programming (NLP) to help you exploit the key learning points from each step.

You certainly do not have to complete all the exercises but just try the ones that appeal. Mental exercises are like physical ones, some seem to work for some people but not for others. However, as you come to understand the rationale behind the various exercises suggested, you might begin to create your own exercises that meet your own requirements.

Acknowledgements

I would therefore like to thank two groups of people:

Firstly those specialists from the scientific disciplines and from the more philosophical traditions whose published work has informed the thinking and concepts found in this book (a reading list can be found in the Appendices which I hope will motivate you to explore these subjects further)

And secondly all those people who have used the self-diagnostic questionnaire to identify their own issues and priorities for change.

I would also like to thank the essential contribution in the writing of this book made by the coffee bars of Portishead, North Somerset and Aphrodite Hills, Cyprus.

Rennie Gould

September 2016

INSIGHT

7 Steps to Self-Awareness & Personal Fulfilment

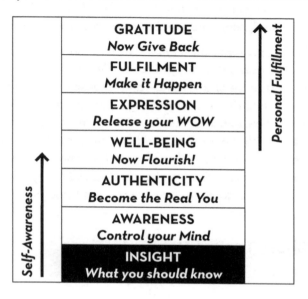

Introduction

This is the first step of our journey towards Self-Awareness and Personal Fulfilment and we need to start it by developing an understanding of how our brain works.

We will discover that our brain runs the show by controlling everything we think, everything we feel and everything we do, but for most of the time we are on Autopilot, with most of what is going on taking place in the dark without us having much awareness of what is happening and why. In this Step, we will learn how our brain was initially programmed and how this blueprint has been added to during the course of our lives to create the person that we are now and how we therefore perceive ourselves and the world around us. We will also learn that everything is stored in our brain through a series of wired connections that are like grooves in the very fabric of our brain, but that these connections can be re-wired or re-grooved.

We will also learn that a unique evolutionary development has given us a get-out-of-jail card called the mind that gives us a sense of awareness and a sense of self, both of which hold the secret of change, providing of course we know how to use the tools. All the scientific disciplines together with the ancient traditions put the mind at the centre of everything and confirm its tremendous powers of transformation. The Insights that we will gain from this step will be fundamental to our progress throughout all subsequent steps.

A Short Tour of the Brain

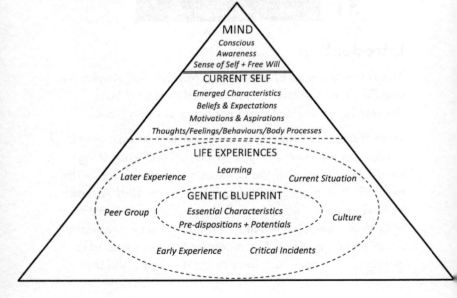

Using the simplified representation above, we will take a short tour of the brain to understand how it all works and how it becomes programmed to create the person we have become. We will start with its essential architecture and then learn how our *Genetic Blueprint* is activated by our *Life Experiences* to create our *Current Self* together with our *Emerged Characteristics, Beliefs & Expectations, Motivations and Aspirations* that determine the perceptions of ourselves and the outside world, which in turn determine our *Autopilot Programmes* – how we *Think, Feel* and *Behave*, and how our internal *Body Processes* work in response. Finally we will be introduced to our *Mind* where our *Conscious Awareness* resides that creates our *Sense of Self* and our *Free-Will*.

Is it a Pyramid or an Iceberg?

Actually, it's both! Firstly, there is a good reason for the pyramid shape as it represents the natural hierarchy of the brain with the higher-order functions of the mind at the top and the other functions nearer the bottom. Secondly, if it was drawn to scale, we can also view the brain as an iceberg with the tip of our mind, together with its unique capabilities, sitting above the waterline accessible, but with the majority of our brain, containing and all of its other functions, hidden below the waterline in our subconscious and less accessible.

Our brain is Groovy

All of our essential characteristics, feelings, memories, experiences, learning, values, beliefs, expectations, aspirations and fears are stored in the same way that information is stored on a computer's hard disk by creating physical grooves in the fabric and structure of our brain.

This is not quite true, as they are not actually grooves, but networks of interlinked brain cells (neurons) that hold all this information, which can then be retrieved whenever we want to access anything, whether consciously or unconsciously, just as we would retrieve information from our computer.

The brain is the centre of everything and the vast number of neurons act like wires to pass signals and messages to all other parts of the brain and then to the rest of the body. If you can imagine a vast old-fashioned telephone exchange with masses of wires and connections all over the place, then this is what the inside of a brain looks like. The similarity with the telephone exchange continues as only some of the circuits in the exchange are live corresponding to the number of calls being made at any given moment. Similarly, not all the brain's circuits are live at any one time as this depends upon what we are thinking, feeling and doing.

Networking for Brains

To continue the computer analogy, the brain has a central processor, operating system and memory storage and it creates all of our thoughts, feelings and actions and controls all of our bodily systems such as breathing and digestion. Anything that holds our attention creates a physical response in our brain and the more attention and emotional intensity that anything creates, the more networks and circuits are formed and the more important this information and these connections become. When something is perceived as exciting for example, a message is passed all around our brain and body to give us the thoughts, feelings and actions that we associate with excitement.

In fact, everything we think, feel or do generates the necessary connections in our brain and with the rest of our body to make sure the right things happen, which has very important implications for what we should allow ourselves to think and feel, but also how we might use this essential connection to pro-actively influence our situation.

Once a circuit in the brain has been activated, it is more likely to be activated in the future and the more often and the more intensely it is activated, the more extensive the circuit becomes, the more strongly the message is transmitted and the more important this memory becomes in the brain. This means that whatever we intensely focus on becomes more important and more *grooved* in our brain. In this way, our brain is like a muscle – the more we use it, the bigger it gets and in the same way that developing our arms or chest makes these areas bigger, whatever we concentrate on becomes more developed in our brain, which implies we can train our brain to get bigger and better in any area we choose.

Michael O'Shea in *The Brain: The brain is not an independent agent, residing in splendid and lofty superiority in our skulls. Rather it is part of an extended system reaching out to permeate, influence, and be influenced by every corner and extremity of your body. Practically nothing is out of its reach. Every breath you take, every beat of your heart, your every emotion, every movement, including involuntary ones such as the bristling of the hairs on the back of your neck and the movement of food through your gut – all of these are controlled directly or indirectly by the action of the nervous system, of which the brain is the ultimate part.*

The Mind – Our Command Centre

Our brain has a number of regions or clusters of brain cells that are responsible for different activities, such as helping us to see, to hear, to taste or to feel. It also has specialist regions devoted to helping us control our *Body Processes*, such as increasing our heart-rate and breathing when we need to run and for helping us digest food and converting it into energy. Most of our body processes run themselves very efficiently without much conscious intervention from us, but as with most networks or complex organisations, there is usually a leader and in our brain this leader is called our *Mind*.

The mind has connections with every other part of the brain and is effectively our *Command Centre*, as it issues instructions in line with our intentions. It can therefore be said that the role of the mind is to *make* choices and the role of the rest of the brain and the body is to *deliver* on these choices.

Every time we concentrate or focus on something our mind brings the brain to attention to await further instructions before mobilising and coordinating any activity across the rest of the brain. This is why attention and focus is so important and is one of the reasons why *Mindfulness* is such an important practice as we will later discover.

There is still a debate as to where the mind and conscious

awareness is located in the brain, but given that many of our higher order thinking and reasoning capabilities that help us reflect, evaluate and make decisions are found in our *Pre-frontal Cortex* (PFC) which is the front part of our brain just behind our forehead, we will assume this is where our mind resides.

The mind demonstrates what is called an *Executive Function*, which means it decides between conflicting thoughts and ideas to select the best course of action and then keeps track of how we are doing against these goals. It also maintains our social control by suppressing any unacceptable behaviour and we will explore the mind in greater detail later.

Rennie: I came to realise that the brain and particularly the mind was at the centre of everything – all roads lead back to the mind – which is the fundamental and common element in all disciplines from quantum physics to Buddhism.

Other Regions of Interest

You might be relieved to note that this is not a neuroscience text book, but there are a few more areas of the brain that we need to know about as they have a major impact on our well-being. Although most of us know that the *Left-Side* of the brain is concerned with planning and details, whereas the *Right-Side* is more concerned with the bigger picture, fewer of us are probably aware that a happy brain is a brain where both left and right sides are largely in balance. When neuroscientists look inside the brain using scanners that measure brain activity, they find that people suffering from low mood and anxiety tend to have an over-active right-side. Could this also explain why highly creative people are often prone to psychological issues?

As John B. Arden says in *Rewire Your Brain: People who are depressed under-activate their left frontal lobes. If you are prone to feeling down, more than up, activating your left frontal lobe by doing something constructive will help you slip out of the chronic low emotional* foundation.

One of the ways to reduce these negative psychological consequences is to strengthen the activity on the left-side of the brain in order to bring it back into balance. This can be done by doing anything constructive such as planning or organising or even by doing something methodical like counting backwards from 100. It can also be done by cleaning out a cupboard or cutting the grass or clearing out your garage. I always wondered why clearing out my old clothes and cutting the lawn made me feel better, so now I know!

Fear and Dread

Additionally, our brain is always on the lookout for danger and has a panic circuit that emerged to respond very quickly to perceived threats. This circuit contains a brain structure called the *Amygdala* that is referred to as the seat of fear and dread. The amygdala is involved in strong emotions and is an evolutionary adaptation that enables us to react quickly without thinking when we suddenly notice an orange and black stripy thing skulking in the bushes, rather than hang around to fully process all the available information and perhaps become lunch.

Unfortunately, this circuit can get over-heated by

preparing us for threats when no threat actually exists which can lead to excess stress and anxiety. We therefore need to calm down this circuit and to bring it back under control and *Mindfulness* is again very important here as it acts like a quarantine area, where we can hold any negative or anxious thoughts to stop them shooting straight through to the Amygdala and setting off the panic circuit. Over the longer term, as the panic circuit becomes less active, it begins to lose its propensity to activate in the future.

Mind-Brain-Body Link

The Mind and Body are inter-connected – one affects the other and vice-versa. So if we have negative thoughts, we feel negative and behave negatively, but if we have positive thoughts, we feel positive and behave positively. Interestingly, this also works the other way around, so if we behave positively, say by smiling or doing something pleasant, we feel positive and have positive thoughts.

This fundamental link between mind and body and between thoughts, feelings and actions, is the mechanism by which we can create our own experience and is the mechanism we will use extensively during the course of this book.

Role of Emotions

Feelings and emotions are designed to strengthen particular types of thoughts so they are more likely to be acted upon. Emotions therefore strengthen the message to let us know when something is good or pleasant that we should move towards or when something is bad and unpleasant that we need to avoid.

Positive emotions include: *Love, Joy and Pleasure* which are supposed to draw us closer to whatever caused these emotions, whereas negative emotions such as *Pain, Anger and Fear* are designed to steer us clear.

These strong emotions can quickly cascade around our body, setting off lots of associated physical effects and manifestations and once an emotional trigger is felt, lots of other associations will flood into our mind. The power of emotion and feeling to bring our whole brain and body to attention will be fully explored in later steps as these tools represents the most effective instruments we have for improving our well-being and for changing our overall situation.

However, there are other emotions that seem to have a less clear message such as *Doubt, Irritation, Frustration, Anxiety and Tension,* which are perhaps signs that something is not right and needs further investigation. Given that our mind uses emotions and feelings to emphasise certain thoughts or to stimulate some action, if we experience a strong feeling about something, perhaps we should ask ourselves why?

Perceiving the outside world

For all we know the outside world doesn't actually exist but is just a figment of our imagination. I apologise for such an outrageous statement so early in the book but unfortunately this is a reasonable conclusion based on the evidence.

As VS Ramachrandran says in *The Tell-Tale Brain*: *The link between perceiving and hallucinating is not as crisp as we like to think.*

One could almost regard perception as the act of choosing the one hallucination that best fits the incoming data which is often fragmentary and fleeting. Both hallucinations and real perceptions emerge from the same set of processes.

Our perception of the outside world is actually created by our mind, by assembling the various bits of information passed to our brain from our various senses in the form of electrical and chemical signals. Therefore when we look at a tree, the message that comes from our eyes is broken down into various signals and passed to our brain which then re-assembles them into an image we call a *tree*.

So we don't actually know whether the tree exists other than in our mind and is precisely why so many philosophers have ended up being a few sandwiches short of a picnic as they have struggled to resolve this issue. Perhaps philosophy will one day catch up with science and recognise we can now look inside our heads to observe what is happening rather than having to merely philosophize about it. Anyway, you might think this discussion about the nature of reality is something of a hypothetical argument with little practical benefit, as we *know* there is a tree out there; it does however raise the question of how we perceive events in the outside world and is an important theme we will revisit many times.

So what is real?

This is course raises another question of what is real versus what is imagined, particularly as our brain has no way of knowing which is which. When we use our imagination to conjure up an image of a tree, particularly if we create intense feelings of green leaves blowing in the wind and the dramatic contrast of the dark trunk against the blue sky, our brain receives exactly the same information as it would if the information had come from a *real* tree.

We are just cutting out the middle man and planting the perception of the tree directly into our brain, if you can excuse the puns. This is not just a nice-to-know academic exercise, as this point is of crucial importance when we start to make changes to ourselves and to our situation, as we are in effect going to manipulate our brain into believing something that might *not yet be real*.

We have a negative bias

We are all programmed to think the worst rather than the best, to be more pessimistic than optimistic and to fear risk rather than to embrace opportunity. This makes us generally cautious, risk averse and suspicious of anything new or different. Why? The answer, as with many other answers, can be found in the understanding of our evolution and its lasting effects. Our ancestors had to contend with a great many more unpredictable risks than we do today – there may well have been a sabre-toothed tiger hiding behind every bush just waiting to feast on an unsuspecting biped who happened by.

Those that survived to produce the next generation were therefore more aware of risk and more likely to scarper at the first sign of flashing white teeth, even though many of these *sightings* were probably false alarms. But here's the point, you can make the mistake of thinking you can see a sabre-toothed tiger when there isn't one actually there as many times as you like, but you can only make the opposite mistake once! Rather fittingly, this is called the *Paper Tiger Syndrome* by psychologists and is why we have evolved to be risk averse.

Load up on positives!

So what should we take from this fundamental insight about our inherent risk aversion?

Firstly, we should remember that as we are negatively biased we could pass up on new opportunities that present themselves and be less likely to push ourselves to our natural limits.

Secondly, we are likely to feel more anxious and fearful than any situation warrants and more likely to have negative thoughts and feelings than positive ones.

Thirdly, we can groove fear and anxiety into our brain if we over-trigger this response mechanism.

Fourthly, as we apparently need at least three positive thoughts to counter the negative ones that tend to stick around longer, we should therefore go overboard on stocking up with good thoughts and memories to ensure we stay in a more positive frame of mind.

And *fifthly,* this negative bias could also explain why we are more inclined to beat ourselves up about negative aspects of our personality and things we are bad at, rather than celebrate our more positive aspects and the things we are good at.

These issues are extremely important, as the more we associate with any negatives in our mind, the more they become grooved in our brain and more likely to become our default way of thinking and feeling. We therefore need to make special effort to redress this natural negative imbalance and is something we will come back to, particularly in *Well-Being*.

The Conscious & Subconscious Mind

Storage and Efficiency

A computer is configured to ensure it has enough computing power and disk space to access its most important information and programmes easily and quickly. Those programmes that need to be accessed quickly are stored in a specific and easily accessible area of the hard disk, whereas everything else that doesn't need to be so readily available is filed away in a separate but much larger area of the hard disk that cannot be accessed so easily.

In the same way, we have two parts to our brain that work together in tandem. The smaller part is our mind with our conscious awareness that allows us to think, reflect and respond to events in real time and a much larger subconscious part where we store those things that don't need to be front of mind.

Two parts of the same brain

The mind, which is in fact a creation of our brain, provides our ability to reflect on our situation and to focus all our attention on a specific task by delegating everything else to other areas of the brain that chug along quite happily in the background. Just think about having a conversation with a group of people that requires us to look, think and talk in real time.

This simple activity requires massive amounts of mental

capacity or processing power, which is currently beyond the capability of even the biggest and most sophisticated of computers. Nevertheless, we can do these things easily by focusing all our resources on the conversation and by delegating all other tasks to our subconscious.

However, all of these *other tasks* are essential in their own right to keep us alive and safe. Our subconscious is therefore not some separate entity lurking in the shadows, as it is often portrayed, but rather an essential part of who we are with immense processing power and capabilities if only we understood how to use them. Given that we usually leave our subconscious to get on with handling everything that is not front of mind, should we be surprised when it sometimes seems to do things we might not have consciously sanctioned?

Completing the picture

In addition to dumping as much as possible into your subconscious, your brain has other tricks to conserve its resources and to cut down on unnecessary processing. It does something called *Filling-In*, where if it glimpses something it thinks it has seen or experienced before, it then fills in the details to complete the picture without taking in any further information.

This saves a lot of time and energy on unnecessary processing and frees up disk space and processing capacity for the priority tasks. As a result, our mind is always trying to squeeze any new event or situation into its previous experience and perceptions to allow us to make quick decisions without waiting for all the available information.

Therefore, even situations that are only vaguely similar to an existing memory can trigger the same response, particularly if the situation resembles a very strong or emotionally charged memory. If for example we have been attacked in the past, we might view anyone as a potential threat and experience fear whenever we see a stranger. Similarly, if we have had financial worries, even routine financial transactions might trigger the same anxiety.

Jumping to conclusions

The stronger the original memory and the emotional feelings that came with it, the more deeply they have been grooved and the more likely they will be triggered again. By watching out for possible problems that resemble any previous experience, our mind believes it's doing us a favour, but this can become counter-productive just as when a car alarm can be triggered by a mere gust of wind.

There are even more important downsides to this mechanism however. Firstly, we tend to see only what we expect or want to see and secondly, we can sometimes jump to dubious conclusions without considering all the available information.

This can keep our experiences trapped within our current range of beliefs and expectations and is also why anything that is completely new or completely outside our current experience might be difficult for us to compute or even recognise.

Our subconscious is on our side

Our subconscious mind never sleeps and is always working

24/7 on our behalf. It is on our side and will do its best to help us optimize our current situation and keep us safe, as these are its fundamental drivers.

As we will discover later in the step, our fully programmed brain contains our beliefs and expectations that create our thoughts, feelings and behaviour, together with the mechanisms that control all of our body processes. All of which will run happily in the background in exactly the same way every time.

Eureka!

Our subconscious mind is also the fountain of all our ideas, thoughts and amazing insights as it is also working 24/7 to implement what it believes to be our aspirations and goals. So unless we tell it differently, our subconscious thinks it is doing us a favour by showering us with all manner of thoughts and ideas that it believes are useful even when they are not. By the way, we might think that an idea, thought or flash of insight just comes out of nowhere, but the reality is they have probably been brewing for some time below our level of awareness before the magic moment arrives.

As EM Forster said: *How do I know what I think until I hear what I say?*

This means that if we want a problem solved or want an idea to break a particular deadlock, we just need to ask our subconscious to work on the problem and to give us the answer when it's ready. So the next time you lose your keys, just ask your subconscious to find them for you and then relax and have a coffee.

This is all well and good and we should thank our

subconscious for looking out for us so well, but wouldn't it be amazing if we could instruct our subconscious to unless these programs are changed focus on producing creative thoughts and ideas that make us happier and support our aspirations and desires?

Old Programs

If you have had a computer for some time, those original programmes that came with it, together with any early downloads, could still exist on its hard disk and be running in the background causing all kind of problems without you being aware of them.

Similarly, a number of programmes that came with your original genetic blueprint or were downloaded during your earliest experiences, could still exist in your subconscious and be running in the background causing all kind of problems without you being aware of them. As it is with a computer, it is probably good practice to clean out any old programmes from our brain every now and again or at least switch them off if they are causing trouble or interfering with the quality of our experience. We can then load new programmes that better reflect our intentions and aspirations.

Plasticity & Change

Just to push the computer analogy still further, the good news is that our brain can be re-programmed. Our brain is said to be *plastic*, which means it can be rewired, reconfigured or re-grooved, if only we know how. Although this plasticity was an evolutionary adaptation to give us the ability to adapt our behaviour in response to new environments, this ability also allows us to make conscious changes to who we are and to our situation rather than rely on our usual responses.

As Richard Davidson says in *The Emotional Life of your Brain: The brain has a property called neuroplasticity – the ability to change its structure and function in significant ways in response to the experiences we have and the thoughts we think. But, the brain can also change in response to messages generated internally – in other words, to our thoughts and intentions.*

Genes

Endless Diversity

Genes are stretches of our DNA that exist in every cell in the body and responsible for operating and controlling all of our body functions. When scientists began the *Human Genome Project* to identify the complete set of genes that make up the human body, they expected to find around 100,000 different genes, which they believed would be the minimum number to explain the complexity and diversity of the human species.

But they had a shock in store, as they could only find around 20,000 genes, about 20% of what they expected. They have since realised that even this number of genes is easily enough to handle all of our bodily functions and although we share about 99.9% of our 20,000 genes with everyone else, this small variation is enough to create significant differences between individuals as it is not usually just one gene, but a number of genes acting together in complex combinations and sequences (called gene expression) that influence the various physical or psychological characteristics and abilities we demonstrate.

The net effect of having a blueprint that has 20,000 building blocks that can be arranged in endless combinations and permutations is they create almost limitless possibilities and diversity. This diversity is very important as it is nature's way of hedging its bets by putting its money on every possible outcome to ensure that at least some of us survive to pass on our genes to the next generation This diversity also explains why each of us are entirely unique and capable of making a unique contribution, which is something we will explore in *Authenticity.*

Rennie: My understanding of genes has answered a question that has always troubled me, which was why I was born into the place and time that I was? I now realise that as my perception of self is created by my mind, which is itself a product of my genes, there wasn't any choice of where I would surface into life.

And because my mind and sense of self is a creation of my genes, I also believe that when my body dies, the essence of who I am dies with it and does not depart for another place. But the bleakness of this realisation can be very dispiriting, which is itself a good argument for believing something more wondrous. But as I am lucky to have children, I have realised that my essence lives on in the genes I have generously donated, although I'm not sure my three lovely children feel quite as positive as I do about their dubious legacy.

Our Genetic Blueprint

Each parent donates half of our DNA and genetic

blueprint, although the half that is donated by each parent is completely random which goes a long way to explain why children from the same parents can be so different. Our genes influence many of our essential physical characteristics and features which is why we increasingly look like our parents when we look in the bathroom mirror in the morning.

This genetic inheritance also influences our physical and emotional pre-dispositions, such as whether we will tend towards being confident or anxious, happy or sad, extravert or introvert and influences the kind of physical or emotional issues we might suffer from throughout our life.

Our genes also influence what we like doing, what kind of job we are likely to have, what hobbies and interests we like, the kind of friends we are likely to have and even who we are attracted to and likely to marry.

However, as we will soon discover, just because we have certain genes and certain pre-dispositions, this doesn't mean they will produce any effect as there are other factors involved.

Rennie: *The importance of our genetic blueprint started me thinking of my own genetic inheritance and how it had influenced my life. I realised I was a mixture of the good and bad aspects of my parents which I guess is pretty normal as far as inheritance is concerned. I seemed to have inherited curiosity and originality from one side and degree of intelligence and determination from the other. Unfortunately, I also seem to have inherited some less positive traits concerning risk taking and constrained aspiration, which reduced my ability to fully express those*

*more positive aspects of my genetic blueprint. I also seem
to have inherited a tendency towards anxiety and low
mood which I have constantly struggled to control.*

Potentials?

It used to be thought that genes provide us with certain
abilities such as whether we will be sporty, musical or
clever, to name just a few things that most people are
interested in. However, it is now thought that genes might
also provide an appetite for certain thing other than just
the advantage itself.

As Matt Ridley says in *Nature v Nurture: Having a certain
set of genes predisposes a person to experience a certain
environment. Having sporty genes makes you want to
practice sport; having intellectual genes makes you seek
out intellectual activities. The genes are the agents of
nurture.*

Therefore sporty people might also have been born with
the motivation to train, musical people with the motivation
to practice and clever people with the motivation to study.
Additionally, sporty, musical or clever parents are more
likely to support similar activities in their children and
are therefore more likely to provide an environment that
encourages training, practice and study. Therefore, as with
pre-dispositions, having a potential doesn't mean it will
necessarily be realised.

Matt Ridley again: *The original genetic differences in talent
may be very slight indeed. Practice has done the rest.
Nurture reinforces nature. So is sporting ability or musical
ability nature or nurture? It is both of course.*

Gene Expression

Although our genes might give us various essential characteristics and certain pre-dispositions and potentials, they are certainly not our destiny as these genes need to be *expressed*; that is, they need to be activated or triggered before they can have any effect.

We could therefore argue that the terms *Destiny* and *Fate* only have real meaning in describing those latent forces that exist within our genes, specifically in our ability to realise our potential and for our intentions and aspirations to create our experience.

Therefore, we might avoid certain negative physical pre-dispositions if we don't smoke, if we keep reasonably trim and if we exercise. Similarly, we might only realise certain potentials if we are prepared to train, practice or study. Therefore our genes respond to external influences that either turn them on or turn them off and these external influences come from our life experiences and environment, but also from what we are *thinking, feeling and doing*. This is the new science of *Epigenetics*.

Nessa Carey in her excellent book *The Epigenetics Revolution*, describes epigenetics as: *The set of modifications to our genetic material that change the ways genes are switched on or off, but which don't alter the genes themselves.*

Which explains why a pair of identical twins, who have exactly the same genes and where one of the twins suffers from schizophrenia, the other twin only has a 50% chance of suffering from the same problem, rather than the 100% chance you might expect. Therefore life experiences and environmental factors are as important as the genes themselves.

Lower & Upper Ranges

But, just when you think you have understood all of this, I'm about to hit you with a further complication: Genes are not just switched on or off, they can also be effectively turned up or down. This means that our genes are rather like those lights that can be either darkened or brightened by moving a dimmer switch up or down. So rather than having fixed values, our genes can be thought of as having lower and upper limits and can operate at various points in between.

This suggests that we should have lower and upper limits for many of our characteristics or capabilities, which we can refer to as our *set ranges*, which for example means that the speed at which someone can run has probably a lower and upper limit (genetic influence) that also depends upon training and nutrition (life experience).

Similarly, our happiness and anxiety can also vary between lower and upper limits (genetic influence) depending, for example, on the stability and support provided by our family environment (life experience). Although we would like to think that we are all capable of being the fastest runner on the planet or the world's greatest violinist, it is far more likely that as genes set lower and upper limits for our individual capabilities and as these limits are different for each individual, we can't all be champion athletes or virtuoso musicians after all.

As Martin Seligman says in *Flourish: Strong biological under-pinning predispose some of us to sadness, anxiety and anger. Therapists can modify these emotions, but only within certain limits as these emotions probably are inherited and therefore are part of our essential make-up. They can therefore only be ameliorated, not eliminated.*

We can all develop and change

But before you throw yourself to the ground in despair, all of us do have the opportunity to operate at the highest level of our capability and to achieve our full potential, whilst operating at the lower end of our gene activation for our more negative pre-dispositions. The fact that we are all unique with a unique contribution therefore means that all of us are able to do something better than anyone else – we just have to discover what that is.

Our life experiences therefore have a crucial impact on how our genes are activated and therefore on our outcome, which of course means we have a huge opportunity to change how we turn out, either by developing ourselves or by learning how to mimic the effect of life experience and the environment on our genes – techniques we will shortly be exploring in the next steps.

Pete: This has got me interested in how I can change my genes and overall direction with the power of the mind. I want to understand this further.

Life Experiences

Our genetic blueprint comes with a fair amount of existing software, a bit like a computer coming pre-loaded with the *Windows* operating programme. However, this blueprint is not yet complete and allows for other programmes to be downloaded during the course of our lives. There are two very good reasons why we are not born with a full suite of software. Firstly it would be a massive programming task to give a baby all of the programmes it will need throughout its life and secondly, this gives us the flexibility to only download those additional programmes that are useful to us, given our particular situation.

So how important are our life experiences and how much do they contribute to who we are? Well, here's Matt Ridley again: *The big five factors of personality: Openness, Conscientiousness, Extroversion, Agreeableness and Neuroticism seem to vary independently. In each case, around 40% of the variation in each is due to genetics, less than 10% to shared environmental influences and about 25% to unique environmental influences experienced by the individual (25% measurement error).*

If we take out measurement error from the above figures, it would therefore appear that our genes and life experiences are almost equally responsible for how we turn out. As far as our life experiences are concerned, these are more likely to have been influential if they were accompanied by our *Full Attention, Emotional Intensity* and *Repetition*.

Our brain is therefore more likely to be influenced by an experience if it grabbed our attention, if it was memorable, if it stirred strong emotions and if it was repeated, as these factors make deeper grooves in our brain and make these experiences more influential.

Early Experience & Critical Incidents

Our early experiences as a child and before our conscious

awareness and critical faculties had fully developed are responsible for a significant amount of our brain's essential programming. As many of our early experiences came from our parents or from those closest to us, it is likely that their beliefs and expectations went un-opposed to become our own. These early experiences are therefore a further source of our characteristics and traits, both positive and negative, and can also be a source of any *Limiting Beliefs* we might have.

If for example we had been encouraged to express ourselves and to take reasonable risks from an early age, we are likely to reflect these characteristics throughout life; whereas if we had been warned to be cautious and risk-averse, we are likely to reflect these characteristics instead.

Implications for life

If we had been praised and encouraged, we are likely to feel more confident about ourselves, whereas if we were often criticised and discouraged, we would have been conditioned to feel very different. Furthermore, the more we were shown love and warmth and caring the more calm and confident we are likely to feel throughout life, whereas if we were starved of this affection, we are more likely to become more anxious and fearful. Additionally, any critical incidents that created strong emotions during this time would have become deeply grooved in our brain to create a lasting impact.

Rennie: I have always been a late developer and was not encouraged to take responsibility for doing jobs around the house and generally had everything done for me.

I'm sure this was thought to be in my best interest but it probably didn't help me to fully develop. At school I was fairly bright but a bit of a comedian which didn't go down very well with my teachers at primary school as they saw my behaviour as being disruptive. I was once made to sit on my own behind the teacher for a few days, presumably to teach me a lesson. Later in life, my sense of humour was not always appreciated and I have therefore tended to reign-in this natural element of my personality which didn't do much for my own authenticity.

Environmental Influences before Birth

Interestingly, there is also strong evidence to suggest that even our mother's experiences whilst pregnant have a significant influence on how we turn out, depending upon the stage in the pregnancy these experiences were felt.

If everything went to plan and our mother experienced a stress free and well-nourished pregnancy, we were likely to be well adjusted, whereas if our mother suffered any physical or psychological issues at particular stages in her pregnancy, we are likely to suffer from certain physical and emotional issues that affect our development throughout our lifetime.

Learning

We continue to learn throughout life and any new skills or knowledge can also become hard-wired and part of our personal repertoire, particularly if subject to emotional intensity and repetition during the learning process. This is why learning should be fun and why creativity in the learning process facilitates better learning.

Similarly, we are more likely to learn something if it is

repeated, as repetition also makes the grooves in our brain deeper. Repetition is usually how we learned our multiplication tables or how we learned to *groove* our golf or tennis swing and why repeated practice in playing sport or learning to play a musical instrument is just as important as so-called natural ability.

Once these actions have been learned or practiced sufficiently, they become *hard-wired* and easily remembered, such as learning how to ride a bicycle. We will therefore utilize attention, intensity and repetition later in the book when we want to make any changes to how we think, feel or behave.

Virtual Learning

Additionally, we also have a category of neurons (brain cells) called *Mirror Neurons* that have some interesting properties. They allow us to feel what others feel and therefore allow us to feel empathy and sympathy for others. This is of course an important aspect of being human and enables us to forge strong and meaningful relationships with others. But additionally, this also allows us to learn what others have learned merely by watching them, provided we are observing with our full and focused attention.

Experiments have also shown that we can for example improve our piano playing by practicing in our mind and by visualizing our fingers move across the keys, just the same as if practicing for real. This is known as *Mental Rehearsal* and our mirror neurons are again thought to be responsible for this ability. Mental rehearsal or *Visualization* as we will now refer to it is therefore important for learning new skills or for making changes to our situation.

Culture & Peer Group

Apparently, it really does matter where we grow up and who we associate with as these factors have a significant influence on how we will turn out. Martin Seligman in *What We Can Change and What We Can't*, advises us to be born into an affluent democracy and to be very particular about who we associate with.

I think the first bit was rather tongue-in-cheek, although we can certainly follow the latter part of his advice. Culture and peer group therefore provide a further environmental backdrop that influences how some of our genetic characteristics will develop.

Later Experience & Current Situation

Any of our later experiences and any aspect of our current situation can further develop our original genetic blueprint or add to our repertoire of capabilities. We can continue to learn throughout life (if we choose to) and if we also chose to expose ourselves to different *Challenges, Experiences* and *Opportunities*, any of which have the capacity to make additional grooves in the fabric of our brain, subject of course to the tests of intensity and repetition.

Our Current Self

We didn't choose

The combination of our *Genetic Blueprint* and *Life Experiences*, produce a seething mass of competing influences that struggle for dominance and for our attention – a real *Smorgasbord* of possibilities just waiting to be served up. Given that we didn't choose our genetic blueprint and that some of our most significant experiences happened in our early years, it could therefore be argued that much of our *Current Self* was formed outside of our control and without our permission.

Many of our potentially conflicting influences are therefore active in our subconscious and often being triggered in ways we might not understand. Should we therefore be surprised that our mind is often out of control, being filled with noise, repetitive nonsense and random thoughts that seem to bubble to the surface without warning? Is it any wonder that our emotions can swing from one extreme to the other, with our behaviour sometimes bizarre and unpredictable?

Emerged Characteristics

Our *Life Experience* means that some of our physical and psychological *Genetic Pre-dispositions* and *Potentials* have been triggered to become established aspects of who we are. Once triggered, they can be further strengthened by emotional intensity or repetition to become even more grooved in our brain, whereas other genes may still lie dormant awaiting their chance to activate.

We may for example be inherently artistic but we might not have been exposed to influences that would have brought this out. We may also be inherently adventurous, but may have suffered some experience in early life that discouraged this. We may also have a genetic pre-disposition towards anxiety or depression which may or may not have been triggered throughout our lifetime. However, as we have previously discovered, we can learn to move towards the lower or upper end of our genetic set ranges that we inherited.

Therefore any potential advantage provided by our genes can be either exploited or wasted depending on whether these genes become activated but likewise, any genetic pre-disposition towards a physical or psychological issue does not necessarily lead to an unmanageable problem, as the impact of those particular genes can be reduced.

Beliefs & Expectations

Another hugely important element to emerge from the combination of our genetic blueprint and life experience are our *Beliefs* and *Expectations*, which includes our *Values*, and *Assumptions*. These are responsible for how we perceive ourselves and the world around us and influence how we subsequently respond. Although we might be aware of some of these influences, others might sit deep in our subconscious and although unknown to us, can still be very influential. Our Current Beliefs and Expectations consist of:

- *What we believe we are good at doing*
- *How we believe the world works*
- *How we perceive events, situations and people*
- *What we expect will happen in the future*

Current Motivations & Aspirations

Similarly, our current *Motivations and Aspirations* have also emerged from the combination of our Genetic Blueprint and Life Experience and here again, although we might be consciously aware of some of them, others might sit deep in our subconscious and yet still be very influential. Our Current Motivations and Aspirations can be described as:

What appears to be motivating us to specific actions

What we currently appear to aspire towards

What overall goals we appear to be aiming for

But it should be emphasised that because many aspects of our Current Selves were produced by the random combination of our original Genetic Blueprint and Life Experiences, and therefore we could legitimately claim that many of our current Beliefs, Values, Motivations and Aspirations may not reflect our true Authentic Self.

Perception Filter

Our Beliefs and Expectations therefore create a Perception Filter through which we view and evaluate the outside world and how we translate these perceptions into how we think, feel and behave in all circumstances:

- We will only see what we want to see,

- We will only believe what we want to believe

- We will only achieve what we expect to achieve

It will be clear that to make any major changes to ourselves and to our situation, we must first change our Beliefs and Expectations and therefore our Perception Filter, otherwise they will cause us to think the same way, feel the same way and to behave in the same way, every time.

The Placebo Effect

If there was any doubt about the power of the mind and the effect of our beliefs and expectations on the reality we experience, we only have to look at the *Placebo Effect*, where our mind and body can be fooled into believing that a treatment or drug contains a wonder ingredient with an incredible effect when in reality there is no active ingredient whatever. Drug manufactures know this effect only too well, as their new treatments must not only demonstrate they have a positive effect but they must also do better than a *mere* placebo.

There are countless examples of the effect of placebo's in the media but my favourite is when a so-called performance enhancing pill was given to a group of international indoor cyclists claiming it would give them a temporary (and legal) lift in their performance. It was administered after their usual training session when they would have normally have been resting from their exertions, but instead they were asked to go back onto the track and to try to set fast times. Most of the cyclists improved their times and some even achieved personal bests, saying could *feel* the difference the pill had made. They were simply gobsmacked when informed the pill was simply cornflour.

Autopilot Programmes

Congratulations, your *Current Self* is now complete with your *Emerged Characteristics* and *Beliefs and Expectations* now fully formed. Your brain is now fully programmed and will happily go about its business as if on *Autopilot*, with your subconscious in control and without any further contribution from you (if you so wish). These all-powerful Autopilots consist of our *Thoughts, Feelings, Behaviour* and *Body Processes.*

Thoughts, Feelings & Behaviour

Unless we are being fully aware and conscious of ourselves and our situation, our autopilots will be in control and therefore any external situation and event will be perceived in line with our beliefs and expectations which will then drive our thoughts, feelings and behaviour without you having to think too much about what is going on. Most of our usual behaviours, habits and instincts will handle most situations without the need for much reflection, which you must admit is a very efficient process, providing of course these autopilots reflect our authentic intentions and aspirations!

However, as well as not reflecting our true authentic self, our current perceptions created by our *Current Beliefs and Expectations* may not reflect reality and can result in the following:

- *Over generalizing*

- *Catastrophizing or all-or-nothing thinking*

- *Taking fixed and unbending positions*

- *Not accepting the evidence but using emotion to draw conclusions*

- *Jumping to conclusions or stereotyping*

- *Thinking it's always our fault*

- *Over-stating the negatives and under-stating the positives of any situation*

These are the classical *Thinking Errors* addressed by *Cognitive Behaviour Therapy* (CBT) which aims to change how we perceive ourselves and the world – to change our *Beliefs and Expectations* in other words.

Body Processes

Your *Emerged Characteristics* and *Beliefs and Expectations* will also drive your *Body Processes* that work tirelessly behind the scenes on your behalf to keep you alive. Your brain will therefore ensure that your perceptions of any situation and your autopilot thoughts, feelings and behaviours will drive your *Body Processes*, using the *Mind-Body link* we talked about earlier.

We don't need to know anything about these Body Processes that are chugging along in the background because if we did get involved, we would probably mess them up. They are therefore kept out of harm's way in our subconscious and respond perfectly to what is going on in our brain and body. Therefore when we feel happy, sad, excited, fearful or anxious, our brain will ensure the rest of our body supports and reflects these emotions by releasing the necessary chemical and electrical signals through our nervous system and blood supply.

- *When we feel happy, our brain releases chemicals that improve our immune system and energizes the rest of our mind and body, but when we feel unhappy, the reverse happens*

- *When we exercise, our brain releases chemicals that make us feel charged and alive*

- *When we feel attraction, our brain releases chemicals of feelings of love and attachment*
- *When we feel threated our brain releases chemicals to prepare a fight or flight response*

The way our brain works ensures our Beliefs and Expectations are being implemented even when we are not thinking about them as they have become grooved in our brain and are constantly working in the background 24/7. Additionally, our subconscious mind will now be programmed to produce only those thoughts and ideas in line with our Beliefs and Expectations.

Our subconscious which is a seething mass of activated and un-activated genes, positive and negative life experiences and long forgotten programmes, will therefore do its best to optimize our situation but no wonder it sometimes behaves like a naughty child, filling our head with all kinds of half-baked nonsense which can regularly have us spinning in ever decreasing circles. Additionally, if we usually operate on autopilot, are we any better than those so-called lower creatures that only act on instinct?

We can therefore illustrate the creation of our *Current Self* and its implications as follows:

GENETIC BLUEPRINT + LIFE EXPERIENCES

CURRENT SELF
(Emerged Physical & Psychological Characteristics)

Current Beliefs + Expectations
(Perception Filter)

Current Motivations Aspirations & Goals

Autopilot Programmes
(Thoughts, Feelings & Behaviour)
(Body Processes)

Therefore, when in Autopilot, we will respond to most events and situations in the same old way, every time.

SITUATION

PERCEPTION FILTER
(Beliefs & Expectations)

AUTOPILOT RESPONSES
Thoughts, Feelings + Behaviour
Body Responses

A Summary

So just to summarise, many elements of our *Current Self* including our *Emerged Physical and Psychological Characteristics*, our *Beliefs and Expectations* and our *Motivations, Aspirations and Goals* were largely created by forces outside of our awareness or control.

If this wasn't bad enough, then it gets even worse, as we now know that much of our *Thinking, Feeling and Doing* takes place as if on *Autopilot* without much conscious intervention. Doh...

The Mind

Perhaps you might be wondering when I was going to talk about that bit at the top of the pyramid that was supposed to give us amazing powers for reflection, evaluation and ultimately change? Well I haven't forgotten, but I first wanted to describe how our *Current Self* emerged largely without our awareness or permission thereby allowing our brain to run everything on autopilot. This has certainly been me for a large part of my life, but more importantly, have I also described you?

Fortunately, we have been given a get-out-of-jail card called *Conscious Awareness*, which gives us the ability to reflect on our situation and to decide whether we need to make any changes and because of its fundamental importance, *Awareness* is the next step in the journey and entirely dedicated to understanding this unique capability.

Class Test

Without re-reading this step, please state which of the following we can change:

1. *Can we change our genetic blueprint?*

2. *Can we activate or trigger our own genes?*

3. *Can we influence where our genes operate within their set-ranges (up or down) and therefore influence our situation in life?*

OK, your time is up. Please put your pens down now and hand your papers to the front. Only kidding, but I've always wanted to say this... Actually, the answers are:

1. *NO* (Although recent advances in genetics suggest this might soon be possible)

2. *YES*

3. *YES*

And we make these changes by:

✔ Having different *Life Experiences* and *Learning Experiences*

✔ Creating new *Beliefs and Expectations* and therefore changing our *Perception Filter*

✔ Creating Different *Autopilots* (Thoughts, Feelings, Behaviours, Body Processes)

✔ Using *Visualization, Repetition* and *Direct Instruction* to program our subconscious

We clearly have a tremendous opportunity to change some of the fundamental factors that control who we are and to influence our situation in life.

Review Questions

The objective of these review questions is not to test your understanding but to allow you to reflect on some of the issues raised in this step and also to help you prepare for the exercises that follow.

1. *Which elements of your genetic blueprint did you inherit from each parent?*

2. *What are your earliest memories or recollections of critical incidents?*

3. *What are your fundamental beliefs and expectations concerning yourself and the outside world?*

4. *How much time do you spend on autopilot?*

5. *Do you feel totally comfortable in your own skin or do you feel there is something missing or not right?*

Exercises

The following exercises are designed to help you experience the link between your mind and body to prepare you for making important changes in later steps.

As was said in the main introduction, you certainly do not have to complete all the exercises but just try the ones that appeal to you.

Exercise 1 - Just Smile!

Settle yourself, take a few deep breaths and then smile. Keep smiling and even allow yourself to break into a laugh if this just happens naturally

How does it feel?

Exercise 2 – Memory

Remember a positive memory or a special place for a few seconds. Fully experience this memory and place again.

How does this make you feel?

Exercise 3 – Subconscious

Ask your subconscious a simple question and then forget about it and do something else.

Did you get a response? How long did it take? How did you receive the message?

AWARENESS

7 Steps to Self-Awareness & Personal Fulfilment

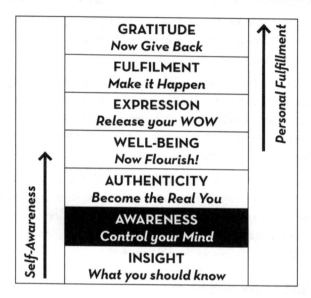

	GRATITUDE *Now Give Back*	
	FULFILMENT *Make it Happen*	
	EXPRESSION *Release your WOW*	
	WELL-BEING *Now Flourish!*	
	AUTHENTICITY *Become the Real You*	
	AWARENESS *Control your Mind*	
	INSIGHT *What you should know*	

Self-Awareness ↑

Personal Fulfilment ↑

Introduction

In this step we build on our understanding of our mind and brain by looking at awareness, which is probably our most important evolutionary development that gives us the unique ability to fully engage with our life experience, but also to reflect on these experiences and our current situation to make whatever changes we then decide to make.

We are specifically interested in how we calm our mind and purify our awareness and will discover that awareness is the antidote of fear, anxiety and tension and can also neutralize any toxic thoughts. We will also learn that awareness is like a searchlight which we can move around at will to illuminate things more clearly and to bring them sharply into focus to heighten our attention and concentration which are the essential prerequisites for re-programming our brain in line with any new beliefs and expectations.

We will find that Mindfulness is a means for maintaining awareness in the course of our daily lives and is therefore an important practice for us to learn. Additionally, we will explore some of the wider issues of awareness and how it influences our reality.

Without awareness, the mind that continues this journey will be a fragmented mind, an anxious mind, a mind that is still in the grip of negative influences that are no longer relevant or helpful and a mind that is always where it shouldn't be and never really present.

What is Awareness?

We are going to talk more about the top of that pyramid or iceberg that we first came across in *Insight*, depending upon how you prefer to visualize it.

An evolutionary development

Our evolutionary journey has given us the highest level of brain function found in any creature on the planet and perhaps the most important is the *Mind* and its capacity for *Conscious Awareness*. Awareness can be defined as our *Enduring Sense of Self* and our ability to reflect on what we are thinking, what we are feeling and what we are doing. This gives us the ability to know who we are, to fully engage in our experiences and then to reflect on all of this.

More importantly, awareness allows us to break the bonds of our genetic blueprint and life experience to not only change our perceptions of ourselves and our situation, but to change our responses to both and therefore represents the most important tool we have at our disposal for transforming ourselves and our life experience.

Conscious awareness and our sense of a personal mind are therefore both creations or projections of a highly evolved brain which means the brain is responsible for producing both. I am aware this might be a controversial statement for those who believe our awareness and sense of self is somehow separate from our bodily processes or derived from an external source, but the evidence suggests otherwise.

The Mind – Our Command Centre

As discussed in *Insight*, the *Mind*, which is the area of the brain responsible for paying attention, concentrating, thinking and feeling, reflecting, evaluating and then acting is effectively our *Command Centre* that brings the rest of the brain to attention before issuing its instructions.

The Mind is the part of the brain we stimulate when we are paying attention and when we are engaged in the present moment, when we are engaged in the present moment and when fully experiencing everything that is happening around us. It is therefore the area of the brain we are using when we are being *Mindful*. This ability to control and focus our awareness is fundamental in achieving a sense of peace and calmness but also for re-programming our brain with any new *Beliefs and Expectations*.

An Exercise

But first a little exercise:

- *What is going through your mind right now?*
- *What are you thinking?*
- *What are you feeling?*
- *Are you in control of what you are thinking and feeling?*
- *Where do these thoughts and feelings come from?*

There are no right or wrong answers to these questions, I just wanted you to start thinking about these issues as they at the root of what we are going to explore in the step.

Lack of Awareness – *Mindlessness*

Awareness has many positive attributes, but it's not a natural state and we can often suffer from the opposite condition: *Mindlessness* which can be defined as an unfocused and fragmented mind that is easy prey for all kinds of random thoughts and feelings, often negative, that can fill our mind with all manner of noise and repetitive nonsense.

Lack of Control & Engagement

In such a distracted state, we are unable to give anything our full attention and our powers of concentration all but disappear. Not only are we unable to fully focus on those positive aspects of our thoughts, feelings and experiences but we are also unable to dis-engage from any negative thoughts, feelings and experiences.

This inability to control our mind has significant implications for how the rest of our brain and body processes respond to this lack of focus and direction and would explain why we might be prone to feelings of anxiety, tension and general unease.

A lack of awareness prevents us from fully engaging with the present moment and therefore from fully experiencing the world around us. In such a condition, we are simply using the present moment as a means to an end – as a means to get somewhere else. Given the present moment is the only place we can ever fully be, this is like mortgaging the present for an unknown future.

Our mind represents who we are and if our mind is continuously distracted and fragmented, we are unable to maintain a consistent and *Enduring Sense of Self.* If this represents your own state of mind you are entitled to ask, just who is it that's going through life?

Permanent Autopilot

In a mindless state, who is in charge? Our subconscious mind will happily run the show with our thoughts, feelings and behaviour on permanent autopilot and subject to an unchanging repertoire that repeats itself over and over again. These autopilots prevent us from fully engaging with the present moment and from enjoying life's rich experience, including potential new experiences, new ideas, new feelings and new actions.

If we don't control our mind, our mind will control us and the only available antidote is to become aware, which brings a number of positives to enhance our experience and our situation which we will now explore.

Rennie: I think I have spent a great part of my mind in un-awareness with my mind full of noise and repetitive nonsense that has prevented me from fully engaging in the present moment. I am generally a tense individual and can quickly get frustrated and irritated with myself and situations. Looking back I feel that I have spent too much of my life somewhere else, almost like an observer who was not really there. I wish I had known a long time ago about how the mind works and how mindfulness can bring awareness to the fore to allow us to fully engage in the present moment. I think it would have made an amazing difference to how I felt and how I lived.

Awareness and Attention

Focused Awareness

The first stage of awareness is created when we hold our current thoughts and feelings in our mind and subject them to our full attention and concentration. The second stage of awareness is created when we learn how to direct our awareness at will.

This ability to control and direct our awareness like a spotlight to either fully engage with anything positive or to dis-engage from anything negative is an important capability that we will explore in all subsequent steps.

Conscious awareness engages our pre-frontal cortex and brings the rest of our brain to attention before communicating specific instructions to the rest of the brain and to the rest of the body. We will come back to this in *Mindfulness* and in later steps in the book when we create specific thoughts and feelings in support of any changes we want to make.

Stuart – I scored very low on awareness which doesn't

surprise me and need to be in better control of where my mind is going more often

Awareness & Engagement

Fully Engaging and Experiencing Life

One of the advantages of being human is our capacity to fully involve ourselves in the world around us and to squeeze all the positive emotions out of this involvement. Without awareness, we would not feel joy, pleasure, beauty, amazement, wonder, excitement, passion, happiness, satisfaction, contentment or fulfilment, to name just a few things.

However, we do not experience these feelings automatically, as it first requires some effort on our part.

We must be in the right state of mind (awareness) to fully engage with the present moment and to open ourselves up to the full range of experiences this engagement offers.

Thoughts & Feelings

A feeling is created when we think of something that has an emotion attached. Therefore a positive feeling is created by thoughts of love or joy, whereas a negative feeling is created by thoughts of fear or regret. Doubts or uneasy gut-feelings on the other hand are usually indications that something isn't right and needs further investigation. As we discussed in *Insight*, thoughts and feelings are inextricably linked and one creates the other. Strong feelings, either positive or negative, can trigger many other associated emotions that can quickly flood the mind and cascade around our body, setting off all manner of associated physical effects.

Tension can therefore lead to more tension, fear can lead to more fear and depression to more depression, whereas excitement creates more excitement and joy creates more joy. Our body will therefore respond in kind to reflect what we are thinking and feeling. Repeated strong thoughts and feelings can then become learned behaviour as the circuits associated with them become stronger and more grooved in the mind.

Joy & Sorrow

As discussed in *Insight*, strong positive feelings are designed to move us towards those things that produce them, whereas negative feelings are designed to do the opposite.

We therefore move towards those things that produce joy, but move away from those things that create pain. Part of being human is therefore the capacity for intense feelings and emotions which allows us to feel the intense highs of love, excitement and passion, but also the intense lows of loss, pain and sorrow. Being subject to emotions is therefore a double-edged sword – if we didn't know sorrow we would never know joy and therefore we can't have one without the other.

Joy motivates us to follow our passions and to become who we should be, by pulling us in the direction of our life purpose. As Joy is a personal emotion, the pursuit of joy therefore expresses and promotes diversity – a key function of evolution. Joy is therefore an adaptation to help us to achieve our full potential and to push ourselves further down our evolutionary pathway. It could be said that we have become *Joy Machines* because joy is a good thing. We need more joy don't you think?

Other Feelings

Other negative feelings such as stress, anxiety, tension, irritation or a general feeling of unease can be signs of a fragmented mind, full of junk or clutter or they can be messages from within, letting us know if we are struggling to identify who we really are and therefore failing to express our true self.

An Early-Warning Device

Our feelings are therefore good indicators of what is going on in our mind at any one moment and can alert us when we are starting to succumb to negative thoughts or to mindless clutter.

Our mind also uses emotions and feelings to emphasise or amplify certain thoughts or events to stimulate some action. As we discussed in *Insight*, we will use this relationship between thoughts and feelings throughout this book, particularly when we come to changing our *Beliefs and Expectations* which is our filter for how we perceive ourselves and the world around us.

Empathy & Communication

Our awareness also creates our ability to empathise and sympathise with others – to feel what others feel and to respond with understanding and compassion. This is another key feature of the human condition that promotes social bonding, sharing and communication.

Thoughts and feelings represent the programming language of the brain and allow us to enter into a two-way dialogue with ourselves, allowing us to communicate to our subconscious and allowing our subconscious to communicate back.

Our thoughts and feelings and the language we have developed to communicate what we think and feel to others is a further evolutionary adaptation that separates us from other creatures and creates our enhanced ability to share, collaborate and to learn from others.

Awareness & Sense of Self

Permanence and Continuity

Our *Conscious Awareness* generates our feelings of being different and unique by creating our *Enduring Sense of Self* that forms a fixed backdrop to our lives.

This sense of self creates a feeling of permanence and continuity from which to experience the world around us – an island of calm in a swirling sea of change – without which our experiences would have little meaning.

Although our memories, experiences, likes, dislikes, skills, capabilities and aspirations may well change throughout life and we could argue we are not the same person at forty as we were at twenty, this enduring sense of self is a necessary illusion to give meaning and context to our lives and experiences.

Without awareness, nothing exists

Without awareness of ourselves, we would not appreciate who we are and what we do and as a consequence our behaviour and lives would be completely meaningless.

Similarly, without awareness of the world around us, there would not be anything or anybody to appreciate what has been created around us. Therefore, to all intents and purposes, we can therefore say that our conscious awareness and sense of self provides a rationale for being and for the universe to exist.

The Ego

Emotions can be negative or positive and similarly, our enduring sense of self can also have negative connotations, particularly if we take this feeling of uniqueness to extremes. It is possible to go so far in celebrating our own sense of difference that we can sometimes diminish the worth and contribution of others. This is the route towards arrogance and ego which will actually distance ourselves from the very thing we are seeking – to fully engage with the present moment and to absorb its many influences.

Awareness & Learning

Grooving New Learning

Our *Conscious Mind* is important in learning a new skill by allowing us to focus all of our attention and concentration on the learning process.

This learning is remembered by creating specific connections in various areas of the brain that stores this learning for future use and every time we practice the same skill, we create more extensive and faster acting networks that effectively *groove* this skill into our brain, which explains why practice makes perfect.

But once this skill is thoroughly learned and becomes grooved in our subconscious mind, it becomes second nature. Therefore once we have learned to ride a bike for example, this skill is stored in our subconscious and allows us to ride a bike at any time in the future without even thinking about it.

As David Eagleman says in *Incognito*: *The goal of any sportsman is to invest thousands of hours of training so that in the heat of the battle, the right manoeuvres will come automatically, with no interference from consciousness.*

We don't have to think about it

This suggests that in order to become really good at something, we must first practice and practice until we can do it faultlessly without even thinking about it, which means that this skill is now totally grooved in our brain and instantly available whenever we need it.

However, once this skill is grooved, we need to keep our conscious mind out of the way otherwise it will interfere with our performance. Try running up some stairs whilst thinking where your feet should be going and you will see what I mean. Be careful...

Awareness & Change

Reflection

As we discussed earlier, awareness gives us the capacity to observe ourselves and to reflect on what we see. We therefore have a unique ability to step back and look at ourselves from an observer position with an open mind.

Not only can we reflect on our own behaviour, experiences and situation, but we can also reflect on the behaviour and experiences of others as if we had experienced the same things ourselves and therefore to also learn what they have learned. Reflection is therefore an important step on the path towards change.

Deciding Between Programmes

A Herring Gull has a genetic drive to incubate an egg, but also has a genetic drive to attack anything red. By putting a red egg near its nest, the poor gull is caught betwixt and between, with one programme telling it to nurture the egg and another to attack it.

As a consequence the poor bird oscillates between doing one thing and then the other and cannot break out of this cycle. Our awareness on the other hand allows us to override our genetic programmes or learned behaviour or to choose between competing programmes by making decisions.

There will be times when we are faced with entirely new situations calling for entirely new actions with nothing in our memory or subconscious mind to help. In these situations, the development of our awareness and real-time decision making come into their own by generating previously un-thought of options.

Free-Will

From this observer position of reflection and evaluation, we can challenge everything about ourselves and our situation and decide whether we want to change.

We can then change our current beliefs and expectations

and the usual autopilot thoughts, feelings and behaviour they produce by consciously creating *new* thoughts and feelings in line with how we want to perceive ourselves and what we now expect of the world around us.

As Bruce Lipton says in the *Biology of Belief: In addition to facilitating subconscious habitual programs the conscious mind also has the power to be spontaneously creative in its response to environmental stimuli...Thus the conscious mind gives us free-will, meaning we are not just victims of our original genetic and early-learned programming.*

We can therefore break free of the bonds of our genetic blueprint and life experiences to change our usual autopilot responses that were mainly developed without our *Conscious Awareness*. Awareness is therefore the root of our free-will which allows us to free our mind and break free.

What next for evolution?

Because our species is relatively sophisticated when compared to other creatures and because evolution is a long-term and gradual process, we can easily assume that evolution has run its course.

Much more likely however is that the evolutionary process is continuing and given that our most recent evolutionary adaptations have focused on our brain and mind and on our ability to shape our own external environment, it is reasonable to assume that further developments will occur in this area.

What additional capabilities these evolutionary developments will bring are open to debate, but it is possible that we evolve more extensive abilities to shape our environment and external reality in line with our requirements and expectations.

Access to the Change Mechanism

We therefore have the ability to re-write, update, change or introduce new programmes of behaviour that are better suited to our environment and also to fine-tune our responses in real-time. If successful, these new responses can then be used again in the future.

Awareness stills and balances the mind and gives access to our current self and its beliefs and expectations, which generate our perceptions of who we are and of the world around us. This access allows us to re-groove our brain by making changes to our sense of self and to how we think, feel and behave.

Sally – I am aware of the importance of being in the present and also have the ability to experience the present but find it hard to stay in it. As an individual, I do think I have a particularly active mind and it can easily run away from me. I certainly find it hard to focus on one thing, rather than just "sitting" with something I often find my mind will start analysing and comparing the situation.

Mindfulness & Awareness

Mindfulness is the antidote to *Mindlessness* and is a means of achieving and maintaining *Awareness* to exploit the benefits this brings.

What is Mindfulness?

Go into any bookshop and seek out the self-help section and you will find that *Mindfulness* has probably achieved the most shelf space, but is it just another passing flavour of the month or is there something more significant and enduring about it?

It might be useful to provide a definition of what mindfulness is, but unfortunately, mindfulness does not lend itself to a slick and all-encompassing definition, so let me give you a number of definitions to see if any one of them hits the spot. *Mindfulness* is:

- *A means of achieving and maintaining conscious awareness*
- *A regular practice*
- *Something that can be learned*
- *A simple technique you can include in your daily routine*
- *A way of freeing our mind of its usual clutter and noise to promote inner calm, peace, tranquillity and harmony*
- *A practice that seeks to control our awareness so that we can focus all of our attention*
- *A way of keeping us grounded in the present moment and focused on the now*
- *A means to fully engage and experience the many wonders of life*
- *A way of neutralizing the negative thoughts and feelings that can affect our mood and dampen our energy*
- *A means to emphasize those positive thoughts and feelings that lift our mood and give us energy*
- *A means of improving our health and overall performance*

- *A technique to help us open up a two-way dialogue with our subconscious mind*

- *A preparation of the mind to create lasting change*

Actually, *Mindfulness* is all of the above and potentially offers many benefits for our well-being, so let's now look at these definitions in more detail.

A means of achieving and maintaining awareness

In essence, *Mindfulness* is a tool for achieving and maintaining conscious awareness. It is therefore an essential technique for ridding our mind of unnecessary clutter and for distilling and purifying the quality of our attention, concentration and focus. Mindful awareness is therefore an essential pre-requisite for harnessing the full power of our mind and for creating change.

Mindfulness is a form of meditation and based on techniques that have been around for thousands of years for training the mind to focus and to concentrate our attention. Mindfulness also reflects the Buddhist notion that everything in the mind is simply temporary and will soon pass and we should not add to our clutter by giving anything temporary any undue attention but to merely become aware of its passing.

A practice to be learned

Mindfulness is a practice which means it's something you have to keep doing on an ongoing basis. It's something you need to persevere with in order to extract its full benefit and is also a technique which means it has to be learned.

The mind must be trained to bring itself back to where you want it to be and so every time you shepherd the mind back to the present moment it is being trained.

Ultimately, you probably can't control the mind, but you can keep bringing it back to awareness and back to focus on the present moment, even if this is a constant battle (as it is for me).

But in the same way as we don't complain about the weights being heavy when we are developing our muscles as his means the exercise is working, we shouldn't worry about having to constantly shepherd our mind back to awareness as this just means our training is working.

A simple technique

The essential strategy for meditation is to:

1. *Relax*
2. *Focus on one thing by really paying attention and exploring it*
3. *If the mind wanders, gently bring it back*
4. *Let everything else go*

Mindfulness is clearly based on this ancient practice, but although a form of meditation, Mindfulness is not necessarily concerned with clearing our mind of everything or about chanting whilst sitting cross-legged in a darkened room, nor is about putting yourself into a trance, nor is it necessarily spiritual, although of course it can also be all of these things.

Mindfulness is a simple technique for developing our ability of knowing where our mind is at any moment and without resistance or judgement, to then gently coax it back to where we want it to be without becoming entangled with whatever was temporarily floating around in our head.

Meditation for the 21st Century?

As we will discover in the exercises, mindfulness can be practiced using simple techniques as part of our daily lives, even concentrating all of our attention on simple acts such as cleaning our teeth or showering is being mindful and therefore a means of controlling and focusing our awareness.

Savouring is another part of *Mindfulness*, where instead of gulping down our food for example, we take slow and deliberate action to really savour every morsel and focus our awareness on every aspect of taste, smell or texture or on the feeling we get from just chewing or eating. Perhaps *Mindfulness* should therefore be called *Meditation for the 21st century?*

Rennie: The very act of trying to meditate seemed to make it impossible to achieve and the harder I tried the less I seemed to be in the right state of mind. In fact, I generally got a pain right between my eyebrows that usually stopped me from going any further. I also found using my breathing as a means to meditate very artificial and tended to get all consciously caught up with my breathing rather than for it just to happen naturally. I thought I was probably not doing it right and gave up.

I found Mindfulness much easier to incorporate into my daily life and I can actually practice it anywhere no matter what I am doing. Being mindful during the most simple of tasks also brings awareness into my life in a very practical way and helps with my focus and concentration.

Calmness & Tranquillity

Most of the time our brain is producing *Beta Waves*, which means the electrical activity in our brain is running at a fast pace, rather like a computer operating at its maximum processing speed. This is very useful as it helps us deal with everything that is going on around us and allows us to jump from one idea to the next quickly and easily.

However, it is sometimes useful to give our brain a rest, by slowing it down and by switching off the noise that continually demands our attention. I should know as I seem to be on *Beta Max* the whole time and this can be exhausting.

A very important benefit of *Mindfulness* is therefore the feeling of calmness and tranquillity it can bring to our mind. *Mindfulness* slows the brain down and allows it to run at a slower speed.

We are in a state of mindfulness when our brain is producing *Alpha Waves*, which are brain waves with a frequency of between 8 Hz – 12 Hz per second. This is when our brain, or central processor if you like, is running slow and therefore more relaxed. Alpha brainwaves occur whenever your mind are relaxed, such as during meditation or when drowsy just before you sleep or just after you have woken up.

Taking a Break

Mindfulness is therefore about relaxing your mind by stopping it from churning things over and over again. If this sounds like something you would find useful, I suggest you pay special attention to the mindfulness exercises at the end of this step. Mindfulness is also a way of bringing your left and right sides of your brain into balance and for taming your panic circuit and has therefore been referred to as a natural antidepressant.

As Eckhart Tolle says in *The Power of Now*: *One day you may catch yourself smiling at the voice in your head as you would smile at the antics of a child. This means you do not take the antics of your mind seriously and you are free of the negative stranglehold of your mind and are firmly rooted in the Now.*

Rennie: It is clear to me that my mind is mainly in Beta rather than in Alpha; that is my brain's processor is running hot for most of the time. This is great for what I do and helps me direct and control training workshops with large, diverse groups of people that can go in any direction at any given moment. It is also great for stand-up comedy (yes, I've tried this) as it allows you to play off an audience very quickly. Unfortunately, it is less good for relaxation, for calm focus and for being fully present in the present moment.

Control, Attention & Focus

Mindfulness allows us to control and focus our awareness and attention on something very specific and therefore brings all of our mental capabilities into one sharp focus.

Our *Conscious Awareness* therefore acts like the conductor of our orchestra – bringing all of the players and instruments together in a coordinated way to achieve the same objective. Without the conductor, the only sound we would hear is the noise that individual musicians make when they are tuning up, which is not particularly attractive or useful.

When we are totally focused on something and giving it our full attention, we can achieve a state of *Flow*, where we are in the zone and totally engaged with our actions to the exclusion of anything else.

To be totally focused on the task or activity in hand not only creates a sense of inner calm, but also improves our performance in whatever we are engaged in. Therefore, in order to get the best out of any activity, even exercise, we must perform it *Mindfully* – we must give whatever we are doing our full attention in order to receive its full benefit.

Associating & Dis-associating

Meditation has traditionally focused on calming our mind by distancing ourselves from normal thoughts in order to promote a sense of detachment from the external world. *Mindfulness* can calm the mind too, but we can go further by choosing where we want this calm awareness to go.

We can therefore choose to associate with good thoughts, good memories and joyful situations to extract their full benefit or to dis-associate from any negative thoughts, negative memories and painful situations if we so choose. In this way, Mindfulness allows us to use our awareness like a searchlight to illuminate certain situations and experiences, but also to turn away from anything we would rather ignore. We do this by choosing to take a fully engaged position for positive elements and by taking a more detached observer position for negative elements.

Enhancing Engagement

By improving our ability to concentrate and focus our attention, Mindfulness helps us to fully engage and be absorbed by the present moment and therefore to fully experience the world around us.

Eckhart Tolle in *The Power of Now*, says: *Your happiness does not depend on some future outcome; it depends upon how you are in the Now. You know that nothing that is real, that is here and now can ever be threatened.*

By reducing the noise and clutter from our mind, mindfulness allows us to be more aware of all the information that is streaming towards us through all our senses and to concentrate on the sounds, sights, tastes and feelings of everything going on around us, thereby enriching our experience.

As Mark Williams says in his excellent book, *Mindfulness: ... when we learn to pay attention, on purpose, in the present moment, without judgement, to things as they actually are we start to see the world as it is, not how we expect it to be or what we fear it might be.*

When we are fully engaged in the present moment we feel a greater sense of being in control of ourselves and of events, which contributes to our overall well-being.

Enhancing our engagement also extends to enhancing our engagement with others and therefore by fully paying attention to whoever we are with, we will surely improve the quality of our personal interactions.

Safe in the now

Mindfulness allows us to concentrate on fully engaging with and experiencing the present moment, where the past has been and gone and where the future has not yet happened. If we can learn how to control our thoughts and feelings, we can always be safe in the present moment where the past can't hurt us and where the future can't scare us.

Typically however, we can become overcome with memories from the past or with fears about the future which can put us into negatives states of mind which prevent us from fully engaging with the present moment. Our old memories can only hurt us if we allow ourselves to re-experience them again in the present moment. Similarly, any new fears about the future can only scare us if we allow ourselves to experience them now. Therefore to rid ourselves of these negative states of mind, we must take refuge in the here and now.

Mindfulness helps us to exploit the fact that our lives are in fact a succession of now's, strung together one after another into the future and therefore allows us to be fully grounded in every moment where everything happens and where everything is experienced.

As Eckhart Tolle says in *A New Earth*: *If your relationship with the Now is dysfunctional, that dysfunction will be reflected in every relationship and in every situation you encounter.*

By accepting where you have come from without resistance, you cease to worry about the past and it therefore releases any hold over your present. By also accepting that tomorrow is yet to come, you cease to worry about the future which again releases any hold over your present. This is the *Now* – a place of safety, where everything happens.

In the Now we are free from regret or guilt about the past

In the Now we are free from anxiety or fear of the future

Neutralizing the Negatives

We all know what toxic thoughts are, they are those repetitive, negative noises in our brain that are like unwelcome guests that arrive without invitation and then refuse to leave. They are the product of an unfocused mind that is out of control, rather like a noisy classroom when the teacher has popped out.

We have three choices when we have negative thoughts or feelings: We can either ignore them, we can get involved with them, or we can simply hold them in awareness.

If we ignore them, they will probably try even harder to gain our attention and may therefore become even stronger in our mind. If we get involved with them, they can set off all kinds of other negative associations that might spiral out of control and create fear, anxiety, tension and even depression, together with the physical manifestations that come with these feelings. We therefore have a third option: We can simply acknowledge their existence.

The Third Way

This means we don't ignore these thoughts or feelings, but neither do we get involved with them, but instead, we simply subject them to the full clear and unblinking gaze of awareness and see them for what they really are – passing clouds in our mind that will soon clear.

Eckhart Tolle in *A New Earth* says: *Just accept the feelings you have. See what happens if you don't mind the feeling, what then happens to this feeling? In other words, if you just accept whatever you feel, without identifying with this feeling, what happens to this feeling? You effectively disassociate from the feeling and view it from afar. You become separate from it and therefore it does not take you over. In this way, you put space around the feeling. You ring-fence it. You put it in a box. You isolate it from your real self.*

When we subject negative thoughts to pure awareness, we simply acknowledge their existence without giving them any further attention and without generating any internal struggle or resistance, recognizing they are merely streams of repetitive nonsense generated by a mind that is out of control.

We therefore starve them of the additional energy they need to take a firm hold or to generate further negative thoughts or feelings that could then cascade through our mind to spoil our mood. Faced with this lack of interest, these negative elements should give up the unequal struggle and simply fade away.

Mark Williams again: *In essence, mindfulness allows you to catch negative thought patterns before they tip you into a downward spiral.*

Ultimately, what's going on in around us is not responsible for our peace of mind or for our happiness; it's what's going on inside our mind that really counts.

John: When negative feelings arise, I realise what is happening and deal with them before they turn into feelings of anxiousness and to give myself time when feeling tired/under pressure to take a step back and think about mindfulness.

Switching off the autopilots

Another way to become *Mindful* is to mount a pincer movement by attacking the other end of the problem, by addressing the *Autopilots* and *Habits* that result from *Mindlessness* or from our lack of *Attention* and *Focus*.

By simply changing some of our deep-seated habits, such as were we usually sit on a bus, or what we usually look at when we are driving down our normal route or even which shoe we would normally put on first, we begin to loosen the hold that our Autopilots and Habits have over us and make awareness more of a habit. Even by asking ourselves whether we are aware or not, actually makes us more aware!

Enhancing performance

There is plenty of evidence to suggest that Mindfulness enhances our performance. This is particularly true in professional sport, where no self-respecting potential champion will now turn up for a major event without their sports psychologist in toe.

Affirmations, Visualizations, and getting in *The Zone* are therefore seen as essential elements in the professional sportspersons armoury. Even our problem solving ability and the performance of our immune system are thought to benefit from Mindfulness Training. It turns out that those chanting monks sitting cross-legged in the dark knew something rather special after all...

Access to the subconscious

Being *Mindful* and therefore reducing our noise and clutter opens the channels of communication with our subconscious mind that is working 24/7 on our behalf to follow our instructions and to deliver the necessary messages to all other parts of our brain and body.

Mindfulness puts our brain into an *Alpha Brainwave State* and therefore creates the necessary conditions to set up this two-way dialogue with our subconscious. *In this state, we are better able to listen to what our subconscious is trying to tell us, but perhaps even more importantly, in this state we can re-programme our subconscious with any new instructions we want it to implement.*

Additionally, to enhance the effect of any *Affirmations* or *Visualizations* or any other activities of the mind, we first ensure we are in an aware and receptive state. When our mind is over-loaded and too full of junk, this simply cannot happen.

First Thing in the Morning; Last Thing at Night

Before you get too excited, I am still talking about *Mindfulness* here and of course we can be mindful at any time and should practice mindfulness as often as possible.

But it is probably better to run your *Affirmations*, *Positive Self-Image* and *Visualizations* just before we sleep or just after we awake as this is when we are usually relaxed and therefore at our most suggestive.

Joseph Murphy in *The Power of your Subconscious Mind* says: *The conscious mind is submerged when in a sleepy state and therefore the best time to impregnate your subconscious mind is prior to sleep or just as we wake.*

In this state, any negative thoughts or imagery that can neutralize your desire and prevent acceptance by your conscious mind, no longer present themselves.

Incidentally, this is why we should awake with positive thoughts and feelings that start our day in the right way and why we shouldn't go to sleep worrying about something as this will firmly plant this problem in our *Subconscious Mind.*

Wider Issues of Awareness

This next section is not really necessary for you to incorporate *Awareness* and *Mindfulness* into your journey towards *Self-awareness and Personal Fulfilment.* However, I believe the wider issues of awareness and their possible implications are worth a look because they raise some important questions about the nature of the self and its relationship to reality.

QUANTUM SPOOKY STUFF

Anything is possible

When scientists explored the stuff from which we are all made they found the atom but then they discovered even smaller particles from which the atom was itself made – the old *Russian Doll Trick.* But the sting in the tail was that these sub-atomic particles did not behave as expected.

They were found to move around in entirely unpredictable ways that defied logic. It turns out that everything in the universe at its smallest scale behaves completely randomly and therefore represents a sea of possibilities just waiting to happen until *something* brings order to this chaos to create the physical reality we experience. This *something* causes the possibilities to disappear apart from the one we experience. Physicists call this *collapsing the waveform*, which must be the biggest understatement ever made.

Particle or Wave?

But hold onto your hat as things are about to get even spookier and I apologize in advance for the complexity of this next description, but rest assured, the punchline is truly mind-boggling.

When physicists were exploring the properties of light, they discovered that if you shone a beam of light through two slits in a barrier, the two light beams that emerged on the other side interfered with each other to form an interference pattern on a background screen.

So far so good as this proved that light was actually a waveform. However, light is made up of photons which are particles not waves, but even when you shoot a steady stream of photons through the two slits, they still behave like waves rather than particles and again interfere with each other to form an interference pattern on a screen, which was a little odd. But then the physicists got even more precise and shot *single* photons towards the slits *one by one*, but guess what? There was still an interference pattern formed on the screen which meant that even single photons went through both slits at the same time and interfered with themselves!

Catching them in the Act

This was beyond all comprehension and sent most physicists looking for another job. Clearly this was not what was expected and even worse, it could not be explained. Therefore, in an attempt to get to the bottom of this strange behaviour, those physicists that were left in the lab came up with a sneaky plan. They would put detectors just behind the slits to catch the photons in the act to see what was exactly going on.

Very clever you might think, but this is where it gets really spooky, when the detectors were switched on, the single photons changed their behaviour and acted like particles and not waves and only went through one of the slits, rather than through both of them at the same time.

As a result they did not interfere with themselves and did not form an interference pattern on the screen. But when the detectors were then switched off, hey presto! The single photons went happily back to their usual behaviour and interfered with themselves like crazy.

You Cannot be Serious?

What all this means is when we are watching (the detectors are switched on) the photons behave like particles and only go through one slit and do not interfere with themselves, but when we are not watching (the detectors are switched off) the photons behave like waves and interfere with themselves. In other words, the photons seem to know whether we are watching or not and this changes their behaviour. Our attention (watching) and our intention (measuring) affects how the photons behave.

Even in a *delayed choice* experiment where special detectors are only switched on only *after* the photon has gone through the slits, we still get the same result. It's as if the photons know in advance that a detector *is going to be used* and therefore behave accordingly. By the way, we observe the same effect if we use atoms instead of photons.

Not just mere observers

We seem to be messing with something very fundamental in this experiment and although Physicists can *describe* what's going on, they can't *explain* it and have largely given up trying. They have simply held up their hands and said, *OK, we surrender!* I urge you to go online and put the words *double-slit experiment* into your browser for the full spooky experience.

I would like to leave the last word on this issue to Professor Jim Al-Khalili, a theoretical physicist, who in his book, *Quantum,* gives us the full scientific explanation by saying: *Crazy, isn't it?*

Do we actually create reality?

The inevitable conclusion is that something very weird is happening that we just can't explain. There appears to be some kind of connection between what we are doing and the result we get. In other words, the nature of our attention and intention seems to change the reality we experience.

Now, just play around with these words in your mind for a while as they have some truly staggering implications. Are you there yet? Yes, its official, we are participators in the universe, rather than just observers and our participation changes the reality we experience. This could have some very serious implications for what our energy might be creating out there without us realising it.

Could it mean that our thoughts, feelings, and intentions are having some spooky influence on our experienced reality that we are not fully aware of? Hmmm...

Everything is energy

Albert Einstein found that a fundamental relationship exists between energy and physical matter and one can be translated into the other at a given rate of exchange. This is like being able to turn our money into apples and then our apples back into money again. *String Theory* has gone even further to suggest that physical matter at its most fundamental level is purely energy vibrating at particular frequencies and what separates one type of matter from another is purely the result of the differences in vibration.

Like Attracts Like?

Vibrating energy creates *Resonance*, which means similar objects with the same internal vibrating frequency will start to vibrate in sympathy if they come into contact with each other.

Could this be the basis for the so-called *Law of Attraction*, where *like* is thought to attract *like* and why positive thoughts and feelings are thought to attract positive consequences, whereas negative thoughts and feelings attract negative ones?

If such a law exists, it probably goes a long way to explain *Synchronicity*, where strange coincidences seem to occur that have no rational cause.

Rennie: About ten years ago I picked up a self-help book largely at random because it had a nice looking cover and the title appealed to me for some reason. I found the book really stimulating but some of the concepts were a bit difficult to understand. I then found out the author had written other books on the subject and thought that some of his earlier ones might therefore give a better introduction to some of the ideas I had just discovered, but it was before Amazon had really taken off, and I wasn't sure which of his books I should read next.

A few weeks later I was in another bookshop in another part of the country, looking for a birthday gift for someone and I realised I might be able to find the book I was looking for but wasn't sure where to look. As I walked around a corner to another section of the bookshop, I walked straight into a small book stand that was for some crazy reason positioned right in the middle of a narrow walk-way and knocked the only book that was on the stand onto the floor, together with the stand itself that went crashing into another display. Feeling rather embarrassed, I picked up the book to put it back on display but noticed it was exactly the book that I was looking for, written by the same author...

Everything is connected

Additionally, results from the *Large Hadron Collider* at CERN, have confirmed that we are surrounded by an energy field that connects all of us to each other and which allows the physical mass that we are all made out of to actually exist.

David Hamilton says in *It's the Thought That Counts: We are all connected by a web of energy. If we move one part, the rest of it trembles. That is why when somebody thinks something somewhere, everybody knows about it instantly.*

Physicists also believe that elements of matter that had the same source remain *Entangled* or connected in some way thereafter and whatever influences one of these elements, simultaneously influences the other in exactly the same way, at the same time, whatever distance they are apart.

Jim Al-Khalili again: *If two quantum particles interact with each other they can become correlated in the sense that their fates will be intertwined for ever.*

Could this be another explanation for coincidence?

Rennie: About a year after my bookshop experience, I was in a bar on holiday in Cyprus and got talking to someone about this and that and she mentioned a book that I should read and wrote the title down on a small piece of paper. I put the paper into my pocket and forgot all about it.

About six months later and back in the UK, I was in another bookshop (yes, I spend a lot of time in bookshops and bars...) looking for a book on an entirely different subject. This bookshop was the biggest I had ever seen and had rows and rows of books on every subject you can imagine. I suddenly remembered about the book that was recommended but of course the piece of paper was long gone and I only had a vague recollection of the book's title. On an off-chance, I went to the cash desk and gave the assistant as much as I could remember about the title, hoping it would ring a bell.

As I said the words, another customer who had over-heard me reached forward to the nearest book to where he was standing and handed it straight to me, saying, "I think you mean this one". It was the book I was looking for...

SIMILARITIES WITH BUDDHISM

All that stuff on quantum physics was very interesting I can hear you say, but what has it got to do with anything? Well just hang on for a bit longer as some thinkers have been here before and have said some very similar things about the nature of the self and of reality.

Nature of the self

Buddhism believes that the only constant in the world is our consciousness, which is why it puts great store on meditation and mindfulness in order to purify and distil the quality of our awareness. Buddhism believes that everything else is subject to change and will soon pass. Even the nature of the self is not fixed but can be changed and even transformed by the power of our own thoughts.

Reality

Buddhism also believes that we create our own reality and experience by choosing how we perceive the outside world. *Meditation and Mindfulness* are ways of controlling our mind and influencing how we experience reality so that our attention and focus can bring about physical change. Buddhism also believes the external world to be an illusion created by our mind and we should therefore regard this world as merely consisting of temporary form that will soon pass, which means we should stop taking it too seriously.

Change

We should therefore give up our futile attempts to try and control something that is merely an illusion that will soon pass anyway, particularly as many of our emotional issues originate from becoming too attached to things that do not really matter. Buddhism believes that we don't need to change the outside world to change our experience, but we should instead change how we think and feel about the world because it is our perceptions that are important in creating how we feel. We can therefore escape our past and influence our future through the power of our mind to change our own thoughts and perceptions.

Interestingly, Einstein, as well as equating energy with physical matter, also said: *Buddhism has the characteristics of what would be expected in a cosmic religion for the future: It transcends a personal God, avoids dogmas and theology; it covers both the natural and the spiritual, and it is based on a religious sense aspiring from the experience of all things, natural and spiritual, as a meaningful unity.*

WHAT DOES ALL THIS MEAN?

Common ground?

It would appear that our mind and its capability for conscious awareness is fundamental to the world of quantum physics as well as being the shaper of our reality in Buddhism.

Perhaps we do have the capability to create reality, or at the very least have the ability to choose our reality from the many possibilities that exist? The inescapable conclusion is that there is another force at large in the universe that arises from our attention and intention, in addition to the other four forces we already know about. This force seems to be capable of extraordinary things, the full extent of which we are still trying to understand.

Still a lot to understand

Although we have undoubtedly made significant progress with our understanding of the world around us, there is probably more left to understand than is currently understood. We have only found a few pieces of the jigsaw and therefore our view of what the complete picture might look like is still rather sketchy.

From the very few pieces of the jigsaw we have, some people might think they can see an Elephant out there and some people an Octopus, but the full picture that finally emerges might reveal an animal the like of which we have never seen before but given that our perceptions are governed by our current experiences and expectations, we may simply be incapable of understanding what is actually out there.

We should therefore be ever so slightly humble when we pontificate on what we think is true and take all our current understanding of the world with a rather large pinch of salt. Perhaps the main implications from our detour into spooky science are fourfold:

Energy is the universal currency of the universe, where everything is made of energy and where every action creates energy

Everything in the universe, including ourselves, is connected by this energy in ways we don't totally understand

Something happens to the infinite number of possibilities that exist in the universe to create the reality we experience

There must be another force out there that we have not

yet discovered that has amazing properties to create reality from possibility

We are involved in the creation of this further force in some way that we don't yet fully understand

Are we the missing link?

Ever since Einstein, science has been trying to come up with *The Theory of Everything* – it has been trying to come up with one theory that can explain both the random nature of sub-atomic particles *and* the predictable behaviour of large scale objects like the planets. But, so far, they have failed miserably to achieve this objective and remind me of those who chase after the ends of rainbows and of those crazed dogs that chase after their own tail but merely spin in ever faster circles.

Even poor old Albert went to his grave not having come up with the one equation that would have been even bigger news than $E = MC^2$, although it might have required a much bigger T-shirt.

Sweden

But here goes, this is my attempt at a Nobel prize... If we say that the random particles that form every atom, that represent the potential to build anything at all, are like a pile of bricks scattered randomly on the ground and a finished house is how all the bricks could actually be put together, then *something else* is required to make one out of the other. What is missing from this scenario is *the builder* that puts all the bricks together in the right order.

Perhaps we are the builder? As it is ourselves, with our intention and action, that effectively tells the random particles (*bricks*) how to organise themselves in the right order to create the reality we experience (*house*). Perhaps scientists cannot bring themselves to accept there is another force in the universe that transmits our intention into reality? Are we therefore the co-creators of reality, with our personal energy being the thing that creates it? Perhaps our mind and its conscious awareness is the *Missing Link* that provides the force that changes possibility into actuality?

At the very least we can say that our awareness and intention, and the mysterious energy it creates, can change our own personal experience, but I suspect we will hear much more about this phenomenon in the years to come and hopefully I will be making that trip to Sweden very soon.

Review Questions

The objective of these review questions is not to test your understanding but to allow you to reflect on some of the issues raised in this step and also to help you prepare for the exercises that follow.

1. *How often are you fully engaged in the present moment?*

2. *How often is your mind clear from toxic, negative or repetitive thoughts?*

3. *How much of what you do is just habit or routine?*

4. *When might you practice mindfulness?*

5. *What is your awareness and intention ultimately capable of?*

Exercises

The following exercises are designed to increase and maintain your level of awareness, so you can fully engage with the present moment and fully savour each experience.

As was said in the main introduction, you certainly do not have to complete all the exercises but just try the ones that appeal to you.

PRACTICING MINDFULNESS & AWARENESS

Exercise 1 - Neutralising negative thoughts or feelings

In this exercise, we are going to hold any negative thoughts and feelings in our awareness and just let them pass. So if we become aware of any negative thoughts or feelings at any time in the day or during any of the other mindfulness exercises outlined below, we should do the following:

1. *Allow any negative thought or feeling to arise whenever.*

2. *Don't try to ignore it or fight it, but just acknowledge what it is and even say to yourself, "Ha! It's that silly old thought again!" And give yourself a little smile, while holding it in your awareness ever so gently.*

3. *Wait for it to pass and then return to whatever else you were doing.*

4. *Keep doing this as and when necessary*

By the way, you shouldn't be discouraged about having to do this often as it means you are exercising awareness and control.

Exercise 2 - Focus on an object

1. Sit in a comfortable position and take some deep
    breaths.

2. Pick something to focus on such as a picture or a view
    or a flower and start to look at it. Really give it your full
    attention and concentration to notice every aspect of
    what you are looking at. Marvel at its simplicity and
    beauty. Let the object take over your experience.

3. If anything else comes into your mind, merely
    acknowledge it and then gently move your attention
    back to your object.

Exercise 3 - Watching your hands

1. Sit down and take a few deep breaths.

2. Look from the very back of your eyes at your hands

3. Slowly turn your hands until you are looking at the
    back of your hands.

4. Look how full of character they are. Notice the
    shape and the colour and the texture and every little
    characteristic of your hands as you slowly move them
    around paying very close attention.

Exercise 4 - Mindfulness of Everyday Acts

The following are those things we would normally do
without thinking or on autopilot. For the next week, try
doing some of them with a sharpened sense of awareness.

Don't just go through the motions and dash these things
off as quickly as possible but really slow down and be
deliberately, paying increased attention to every action
to watch how your body is moving and to be aware of any

feeling or sensation that arises. Really luxuriate in the physical experience that some of these actions create.

If anything else comes into your mind, merely acknowledge it and then gently move your attention back to your object

Every now and then pause and take a few deep breaths and feel yourself being fully present and paying attention to what you are doing.

- *Cleaning your teeth or brushing your hair*
- *Taking a shower or a bath*
- *Preparing a meal*
- *Dressing*
- *Cleaning*
- *Pick your own activity (Go on, use your imagination...)*

Exercise 5: Catch yourself being aware

At certain times in the day, become still, take some deep breaths and ask yourself if you are being aware and fully present. By asking yourself this very question, you will actually produce the result you want

MINDFUL ACTIVITY

These exercises allow us to pay attention to what our bodies are doing to reinforce their positive effect, such as imagining what those weights are doing for us when we lift them.

Exercise 6: Mindful Walking

1. *When you are walking, really pay attention to how your body is moving. How your arms are swinging and how*

your feet are moving across the ground.

2. Be aware of the rhythm of your walking and fully engage with this experience.

3. Be aware of the sounds you can hear around you. Recognise them and name them, spending a second or two really focusing on each sound.

4. Feel the air on your face or the breeze.

Exercise 7: Mindful Writing

1. Very deliberately take a piece of paper and a pen and place the paper very carefully in front of yourself and deliberately write today's date in full at the top of the paper.

2. Now start writing. Write about whatever comes into your head. Let your mind just flow without restriction. Write for as long as you like.

3. Write very slowly and very deliberately, paying very close attention to your hand and pen moving slowly across the page. Watch each letter and word being miraculously formed.

4. Really savour and luxuriate in the experience. If anything else comes into your mind, merely acknowledge it and then gently move your attention back to your object

Exercise 8 – Mindful Stretching

1. Stand straight with your feet at shoulder width with your arms hanging down

2. Take a few deep breaths

3. *Slowly raise both arms to point straight up towards the sky.*

4. *Hold this position. Feel the stretch. Pay attention to how your body is feeling.*

5. *Now slowly bring your arms down so they are now level with your waist and pointing away from your sides. Watch your arms move very carefully and feel the movement. Now feel your arms as they strain a little with the effort.*

6. *Slowly bring your arms back down to your sides and take some more deep breaths*

7. *Continue any other stretch but really be aware of what your body is doing and fully experience the feeling.*

8. *If anything else comes into your mind, merely acknowledge it and then gently move your attention back to your activity*

Exercise 9 - Any Deliberate Action

1. *Take a few deep breaths Pick any action and take it slowly, being very focused and deliberate in whatever you are doing. Pay attention to what you are feeling and notice everything.*

2. *If anything else comes into your mind, merely acknowledge it and then gently move your attention back to your object*

Exercise 10 - Challenging the Autopilots

As we have learned, our autopilots drive our thoughts, feelings and behaviour and perhaps we should switch them off every now and again? Switching off the autopilots automatically creates awareness so see what you can come up with

Can I therefore suggest that you do some of the following and see what happens.

1. *Break a habit or a routine such as where you would normally sit or what order you get dressed or anything that is routine*

2. *Try something new on a menu rather than eat what you would always eat*

3. *Walk or drive a different route to work*

4. *Watch a film that you would not normally watch*

5. *Read the kind of novel you would normally not bother with*

AUTHENTICITY
7 Steps to Self-Awareness & Personal Fulfilment

		Personal Fulfilment
	GRATITUDE *Now Give Back*	
	FULFILMENT *Make it Happen*	
	EXPRESSION *Release your WOW*	
Self-Awareness	**WELL-BEING** *Now Flourish!*	
	AUTHENTICITY *Become the Real You*	
	AWARENESS *Control your Mind*	
	INSIGHT *What you should know*	

Introduction

During this Step, we are going to bring together what we learned in Insight and in Awareness to discover who we really are and to use this knowledge to begin to make the changes we want to make.

Authenticity is therefore about knowing your inner-self: What you are about, what gives you pleasure and satisfaction, what draws your interest and drives you forward. But authenticity is not just about knowing who you are but also about being who you are.

Throughout this Step we are going to adopt a positive

philosophy by focusing on the positive aspects of our personality and situation, rather than dwelling on any negatives. Additionally, we will not look to make any compromises at this stage, nor should we be too concerned with what others might think or say, as we need to listen to ourselves first. If need be, we will make any necessary compromises and address any residual issues later in the process.

Authenticity is ultimately about being who you should be and therefore from now on, it will be your Authentic Self that will engage in the present moment to fully experience life.

Authenticity

There are certain times in our lives when we feel engaged, passionate, committed, enthralled and motivated. In this state we feel more absorbed, more energized and more joyful. We are in *The Zone*, where the concept of time disappears to leave us cocooned in a world of our own, impervious to anything else going on around us. This is what *Authenticity* feels like. Have you ever been there?

As Mihaly Csikszentmihalyi says in *Flow: We have all experienced times, when instead of being buffeted by anonymous forces, we do feel in control of our actions, masters of our own fate. On the rare occasions that this happens, we feel a sense of exhilaration, a deep sense of enjoyment that is long cherished and that becomes a landmark in memory for what life should be like.*

Life gets in the way

These peak experiences are memorable because they

represent our highest state of being; unfortunately, they are also memorable because they are relatively rare. Nevertheless such experiences are hugely significant as they represent our *Authentic Selves* in full flow.

These peak experiences often occur by accident rather than design, which is again hugely significant as it suggests the combination of our *Life Experience* and *Current Situation* have yet to create the right conditions for us to experience them more often.

Additionally, the practicalities of life often seem to get in the way – our need to earn money, to provide for a family or to confirm to other people's or society's expectations, can result in us losing track of who we really are. It might also be the case that physical or psychological issues are also constraining us in some way. Therefore, for all these reasons, we might find ourselves living a less than authentic life.

No individuation

Without *Authenticity*, we have not yet become who we are supposed to be, nor are we doing what we should be doing. We are therefore still in development or a work-in-progress, usually living our lives through out-dated beliefs, expectations and autopilots.

The founder of analytical psychologist, *Carl Gustav Jung* had a lot to say on this subject, reckoning that a lack of *Self-Awareness* and *Authenticity* and its consequent impact on our sense of purpose and direction, was a major cause of most of the psychological problems he saw as a clinical psychologist.

Jung would say that most of his patients had not yet

individuated; that is they had not yet fully developed into the person they were supposed to be and were suffering from numerous emotional and psychological problems as a result.

Was Jung Right?

Release Your WOW! will take a leaf out of Jung's book and take the view that many of our run-of-the-mill emotional or psychological problems might just fade into the background if we were more confident in who we are, with the courage to be ourselves without doubt or fear.

Typical *Negative Emotions* such as a *Lack of Confidence, Low Self-Esteem, Tension, Frustration* and *Anger* might well diminish if we had a stronger belief in ourselves and in our own *Sense of Purpose*. This is very much the philosophy we follow throughout the *7-Steps* and we will check at the end of the process whether this has worked for you.

No Compromises

If we haven't established our own *Authentic Sense of Self*, we will tend to respond to other people's agendas and wishes instead of our own. We will find ourselves buffeted by life events, rather like a cork bobbing around in the ocean, being pushed this way and that by the various tides and currents that come along, rather than sailing off in our own chosen direction.

Inevitably, life contains a number of compromises and at some stage we may need to make some of our own to win support or to accommodate the wishes of people we care about. But until we have become authentic and confident in our own sense of purpose, we should resist the temptation to make any compromises or to accommodate other people's wishes or agendas before we are ready.

Authenticity comes first

Any meaningful compromise must therefore take place from a firm foundation of our own authenticity and from our feelings of inner strength that this creates, rather than from anyone else's idea of who we should be. We might also have to manage resistance from those who have grown used to the person we had become and who might feel threatened by changes that threaten the status quo.

We will return to compromise and any remaining negatives or limiting beliefs in *Fulfilment*, but until then, we will focus on ourselves. Without a strong view of who we really are, we can also spend most of our time in our default brain mode and at the mercy of our *Autopilot Thoughts, Feelings* and *Behaviour*, or be driven by *Habit* and *Instinct*. This is not a good place for us to be, particularly as we have the option to take control of who we want to be.

Rennie: I always had the feeling there was something missing as I never felt truly contented or happy. I'm pretty sure that in my case this was down to a lack of awareness and a lack of authenticity (as my own questionnaire results confirm). These insights started me down the road to self-awareness.

Acceptance

We accept who we are & where we are for now...

As a prelude to making any lasting changes, we must

embrace the concept of *Acceptance*, by accepting *who we are and where we are for now*. We are not meekly giving in but we must start from somewhere and what better place is there to start than from our current situation in life? This gives us a fixed point from which to move forward and to make whatever changes we want to make.

Our understanding that we are a combination of our *Genetic Blueprint* and *Life Experience* helps us to accept who we have become and to forgive ourselves for many of our shortcomings. In the same way that it wouldn't make any sense to beat ourselves up for being short or for having blue eyes instead of brown, we should therefore accept all of our *Essential Personal Characteristics* and *Life Experience* that have made us who we are, even the ones we might not like – at least for now.

Rennie: My brain works differently to most peoples. It doesn't go in a straight line but goes whoosh, all over the place. This makes be really good at handling lots of ideas and concepts at the same time and I'm often asked to give funny speeches at birthdays and to create mini-plays and shows for parties, but I would never be asked to organise the event itself. I used to feel bad about my shortcomings but now realise I am what I am and have learned to exploit and celebrate my good points whilst accepting my less positive ones.

Being kind to ourselves

Although it can be fun and instructive to try to identify from the mix of *Genes* and *Life Experiences* all the reasons why we arrived at this point, we don't actually need to do this to move on, *Acceptance* is sufficient. Acceptance doesn't mean rolling over and doing nothing about it, but it means acknowledging:

- *Who we have become*
- *Where we have come from*
- *Where we are now*

Without continually beating ourselves up over those things we might not like.

An end to Negative Energy

In order to move forward, we need to be in a peaceful and positive state of mind to allow our *Conscious Awareness* to reflect on our situation and to focus on the changes we want to make to our sense of self and to our situation. Negative energy and negative emotions are therefore counter-productive and must be neutralized, otherwise what we resist, persists!

Acceptance, keeps negative energy and negative emotions in check to provide the positive breathing space we need. Acceptance brings an end to struggle and resistance and the inevitable cascade of further negative emotions that these feelings would otherwise trigger.

Eckhart Tolle in *A New Earth*: *This is why, by letting go of inner resistance, you often find circumstances change for the better. Surrender, one could say, is the inner transition from resistance to acceptance, from "no" to "yes".*

A Learning Exercise

We must therefore take a positive view of our lives up to this point and accept that who we have become and everything that has gone before is part of our current legacy – some of it positive and some of it less so. We should therefore view our past as a learning exercise and accept that everything has happened for a reason even though these reasons may not yet be fully understood.

Additionally, we should resist our tendency to compare ourselves with others, particularly if these comparisons are unfavourable as envy, jealousy, and anger are significant sources of negative energy. If instead, we are able to celebrate the success and achievements of others, we are more likely to create the positive conditions necessary for our own achievement.

Stuart: I need to strengthen the sense of my authentic self which should be more grounded in the present moment. I also need to celebrate other people's successes more rather than begrudge their success because of my own shortcomings

Forgiveness & Confession

Forgiveness is a very positive emotion, whether it is to forgive others or to forgive ourselves, as it can neutralise those strong emotional traces that would otherwise remain in the background but ever ready to rear their ugly head to cause us pain or grief. This means we should stop giving ourselves a hard time and beating ourselves up for those things we are not good at or when we feel inadequate.

A useful technique to use at this stage is the *Confession*. This is where we finally admit to *ourselves* who we really are, warts and all. This act of admitting something we would rather not hear, even if only to ourselves, can be very painful but ultimately very liberating.

This is not an excuse for continuing to do the wrong thing, but to accept what has passed, to learn from it and to move on.

Acceptance can be tough

Acceptance might force us to confront those things we would rather not confront, to address those things we would rather not address and to admit those things we would rather not admit.

But sticking to our positive philosophy, we are not looking to unearth every negative we can think of, nor are we going to dwell on them unnecessarily, but we are simply going to acknowledge those negative aspects of ourselves to finally get them out of the way.

We should at this point remember our fundamental *Negative Bias* and our tendency to focus on the negatives rather than the positives which means we are likely to overstate our negative feelings about ourselves or any negative experiences. Nevertheless, *Acceptance* can still be very tough as we peel away the layers of veneer to reveal who we really are.

Acceptance may also mean going quite a few steps backwards before we can start moving forward again, which is a little like learning a new tennis or golf swing, where you might play worse for a while until you start getting better as the improved technique kicks in.

Phil: I have definitely learned to be more at peace with myself and have accepted who I am and as a result I have come to like who I am as a person

Uniqueness

Miracles of Evolution

We are all miracles of evolution and success stories in our own right. The genes we acquired from our parents have already had a long a tortuous journey throughout many generations, twisting this way and that to withstand the unpredictable environment and surviving its many threats. For our genes to have come this far is surely worthy of celebration?

Every human being that ever walked the planet is utterly unique. Why? Because no two people share the same combination of *Genetic Blueprint* and *Life Experience*. Even identical twins, with the same *Genetic Blueprint*, have different life experiences that bring out unique elements of their physical or psychological make-up to make them significantly different in some way.

A Unique Purpose

It is therefore only a matter of logic to say that as we are all unique, we all must also have a unique purpose and contribution to make.

There are those amongst us who are very clear about what this unique purpose and contribution should be, but there are many others who have yet to find this out and incidentally, until relatively recently, I would have put myself in this latter category.

In the same way that we all have a unique purpose and contribution, we also have a unique opportunity to experience life to the full and to exploit all our opportunities for joy and fulfilment. We could even say that the future development of our species depends upon all of us exploiting our uniqueness contribution and pushing the boundaries of what we are all capable of achieving.

Discovery

Untangling the Smorgasbord

As we have already said, we could spend a long time trying to disentangle the smorgasbord and trying to isolate the separate influences from the mash up of our *Genetic Blueprint* and *Life Experiences* to identify all the various programmes still running in the background.

This could be an interesting exercise, but in our journey towards *Self-Awareness* and *Personal Fulfilment* we are taking a positive approach by accepting who we are before making changes to reflect who we would rather be. We will then re-groove our brain with any new programmes that better reflect this new self and to ensure these more positive programmes take over from the old ones.

Epigenetics

If you remember our discussion about genes in *Insight*, you will remember that our 20,000 genes that are responsible for everything in our body can either be fully turned on or fully turned off, or set at any point in between. These genes also act in many different combinations and permutations to offer almost endless complexity and diversity.

And as we have already discovered, our genes are activated by our *Life Experience* and *Current Situation* in a process called *Epigenetics* to create our *Current Self* and given that our brain finds it difficult to distinguish between fact and fiction, we can therefore mimic this *external* influence by *internally* influencing our genes in the way we want. Yes, it's official; we can influence our own genes!

Which means that although we all have roughly the same genetic keyboard, we are all capable of producing very different music depending on which notes we actually play and how hard we strike the keys. We therefore have a massive opportunity to change who we are by manipulating our own genes to operate at the more positive ends of their set ranges.

So now comes the $64,000 question:

Are you comfortable with your Current Self and Current Life Situation?

I am effectively asking whether you are happy with the combination of your:

- *Emerged characteristics*
- *Current beliefs, values, expectations and perception filter*
- *Current motivations, aspirations and goals*
- *Current autopilot programmes (feelings, thoughts and behaviour)*
- *Current life situation*

Given that most of these elements were formed by the random combination of genes you inherited and the somewhat random influence of your life experience, I think we are justified in taking a fresh look at these things, don't you think?

Identifying Our New Authentic Self

We now have the opportunity to identify our *New Authentic Self* by considering the questions that follow. The answers will not just come out of thin air, but are often messages from partially activated genes and are therefore flickers of our real self that have not yet been fully expressed.

Key Attributes – *What are we particularly good at?*

Likes & Satisfactions – *What do we particularly love doing?*

Values & Beliefs – *What are the most fundamental aspects of our existence?*

Peak Experiences – *What experiences have given us the greatest excitement and joy?*

Achievements – *What achievements give us the most pride and satisfaction?*

Heroes – *Who do we respect and admire?*

Motivations – *What drives us forward?*

Aspirations – *What ideas and day-dreams set our imagination ablaze?*

Friends – *What do our friends like about us?*

Advice – *What advice or help is asked of us?*

Note: These questions are expanded in the Exercises.

Dislikes

Interestingly, our dislikes can also be important in helping us identify our Authentic Self as they are often the flip side of our likes, because when we feel uncomfortable, irritated or angered by something, this can be due to our fundamental beliefs or values being offended in some way.

Character Strengths

I would also strongly suggest that you complete the *VIA Survey of Character Strengths Questionnaire* that you can find online at *Authentic Happiness*. There are a range of other questionnaires available on this site that will give you some essential insights.

If and when you complete the Character Strengths Questionnaire, please list your top six *Signature Strengths* and for future reference, also make a note of your bottom six strengths or *Signature Weaknesses* as I like to call them.

Becoming Your Authentic Self

TOOLS OF CHANGE

We have now discovered all the information we need to move forward to create our *New Authentic Self* that reflects those aspects of ourselves we want to recognize and emphasize from now on. It might therefore be a good time to understand how we are going to use the tools available to make the changes we want to make.

If we look at all the tools of change used in *Psychology, CBT, NLP, Hypnosis* and *Positive Thinking*, they all have one essential aspect in common – they all seek to make sustainable changes to *how we perceive ourselves and the world around us*. As we now know, this is the essential mechanism, via gene expression, by which we use our mind to re-program our brain and body in line with our new requirements and expectations.

Attention, Intensity & Repetition

We also know from *Insight* that *Attention, Intensity* and *Repetition* are required to re-configure our brain to make the necessary changes:

Attention to activate our mind and to focus it on what we want to achieve to bring the rest of the brain to attention and await further instructions.

Intensity and Repetition to increase the strength of the change message and to create more extensive brain networks in support of this message.

Some of the most important techniques for making these changes are *Affirmations, Visualizations and Direct Instruction* as they directly access the principal mechanisms of change.

Affirmations

An *Affirmation* is a statement that puts into powerful words what we want to believe about ourselves and what we want to happen in the future. But, you have to believe the words and they have to work for you, because it's all about how they make you feel. If you can feel a sense of excitement when you say your *Affirmations*, then they are right for you.

But if you feel they are not right, just play around with others until they do and don't worry about what other people might think about your form of words as they are your affirmations, not theirs.

Affirmations usually start with an "I am statement", to emphasize that the quality or attribute named actually exists now, such as:

I am creative...

I am kind...

I am healthy...

These *Affirmations* should be relatively easy to believe and say as they reflect the *facts* about who you are and if you can say your Affirmations without thinking, this is probably an indication they have been grooved and accepted by our unconscious mind and are therefore working 24/7 in the background. If we find it hard to commit our affirmations to memory, this could be a sign that they are the wrong ones or not believed by our subconscious.

Visualizations

As discussed in *Insight*, the brain cannot tell the difference between something real and something imagined, therefore if we can see ourselves doing something in our mind's eye, this should be as powerful as if we were actually doing it.

Visualizations are therefore an imaginary state we create in our mind or a vision of something as if it was really happening and therefore represent the most powerful technique we possess for re-programming our beliefs and expectations to create those subsequent *Thoughts, Feelings* and *Behaviours* that are the real drivers of change.

As David Hamilton says in *It's the Thought That Counts: In a real sense, feelings accelerate the creation of matter.*

The best way to visualize something is to generate a feeling of what this would feel like and to be excited by feeling this now. The best way to create life changes are to generate excited feelings of how this would feel.

The stronger the visualization the stronger the effect

These *Visualizations* are usually visions of ourselves being the person we want to be and doing the things we intend to do and are therefore fully reflective of our *New Authentic Self*. If a particular visualisation doesn't create excitement, then it's either a weak visualization or it does not reflect our new authentic self and we should create a more powerful one.

We must also try to use all of our senses in these *Visualizations* as the stronger the feeling the stronger the effect and the more likely this feeling will groove itself in our brain to ultimately change our thoughts, feelings and behaviour.

Joseph Murphy again: *Your subconscious accepts what you really FEEL to be true, not just idle words or statements.*

We must therefore imagine what these *Visualizations* sound like, feel like, taste like and therefore create as much excitement as we can to stimulate those brain networks to form and to strengthen.

Rennie: I find it easy to use an affirmation to confirm something that already exists such as a Key Attribute, but I always had difficulty using affirmations that state that something has already happened (as we are often advised to do by other self-help writers) because I know it's not true and I therefore can't believe it's true. However,

I find that visualizations of the future are much easier to believe and they have the added benefit of producing that all important feeling that is necessary to create any significant change.

Direct Instruction

We can even try to re-program our subconscious by giving it a direct instruction by telling it what we want it to do. We could for example say: *From now on, I would like you to accept my new positive self-image which contains all my key attributes, essential values, motivations and aspirations as my new authentic self, which should now influence everything I do.* Just try it and see what happens.

CREATING A NEW PERSONAL PROFILE

It is now time to put together all of those elements that now represent our *New Authentic Self.* We can create a *New Personal Profile*, or a new personal biography, that encapsulates all of these new facets of our new authentic self.

Key Attributes & Essential Values

An essential part of this new profile is a statement of our *Key Attributes & Essential Values:*

- *What we are particularly good at*

- *Those things that are most important and fundamental to our existence*

Authentic Motivations & Aspirations

We can now list our *Authentic Motivations and Aspirations* rather than the ones we were largely following by default as part of our former self.

- *What we particularly love doing*

- *Those experiences that have given us the greatest excitement and joy*

- *Those achievements that give us the most pride and satisfaction*

- *Those things that drive us forward*

- *Those ideas and day-dreams that set our imagination ablaze*

You have probably noticed that we have not yet talked about *Personal Goals*. That is because we are going to look at these in more detail *in Well-Being*, when we apply all aspects of our *New Authentic Self* in the various areas of our life.

Manipulating Emerged Characteristics

In *Insight* we discussed the emergence of our personal characteristics from the combination of our Genetic Blueprint and Life Experience and the fact that we might want to enhance certain of these characteristics whilst minimising the impact of others. We now have the opportunity to do exactly that and to take advantage of our ability to manipulate these characteristics within their set limits.

CREATING A NEW POSITIVE SELF IMAGE

We can now create a *New Positive Self-Image* of our *Authentic Self* using *Affirmations & Visualizations*.

This is probably the most important element in the whole 7-Step Process and fundamental to every other change we will make to our situation in life.

In essence we will create a vision of ourselves in our

minds-eye of our *New Authentic Self* – a very positive image of ourselves looking confident in the knowledge of who we are and what we will soon be capable of achieving.

This new *Positive Self-Image* should therefore contain all the positive aspects of our *New Personal Profile* so that we can carry all of these positive attributes into the future to help us achieve *Personal Fulfilment*.

We are therefore exploiting that characteristic of our brain we discussed in *Insight*; that is our ability to change ourselves and our situation by manipulating our brain into accepting that our new Authentic Self is now *real*.

Due to its fundamental importance, you might want to try this exercise now.

1. *Create a new self-image of your authentic self, complete with all of your positive elements you have identified in your personal profile. You can see yourself smiling, confident and totally at ease with the world. Really luxuriate in this image and let it wash through you and over you.*

2. *Now let this image of your new authentic self get smaller and smaller until all that is left of it is a small sparkling dot that hovers just in front of you.*

3. *Now break your concentration for a second or two by thinking of something else*

4. *Now bring an image of your current self to mind, before you discovered your new self and place the small sparkling dot of your new image right in the middle and let this new sparkling dot get larger and larger until it completely overwhelms your first image*

5. *Now break your concentration again and think of something different*

6. *Continue this exercise until you think it is complete*

Starting Over

All the work we have done to accept who we are, to neutralize our negative thoughts, to more fully engage in the present moment and to identify all those elements of our New Authentic Self, gives us a unique opportunity to wipe the slate clean and to start over. Whatever has happened before is in the past and the future is waiting to emerge and therefore by going forward from this point with new energy, new beliefs and new confidence, we can begin to create a very different life.

CHANGING BELIEFS & EXPECTATIONS

We know how important our *Current Beliefs and Expectations* are as they hold the key to how we perceive ourselves and the world around us and how we subsequently respond. They also hold the key to what we expect to achieve.

As our current Beliefs and Expectations were largely created by influences outside of our control, we could therefore say that many of our current thoughts, feelings, behaviours and body responses, that represent our *Autopilot Programmes*, do not reflect who we really are. As a consequence, that all-important energy going into the outside world is not our true *Authentic Energy*.

New Thoughts, Feelings & Behaviour

Therefore, in order to become our *Authentic Self*, it is imperative that we change our current Beliefs and

Expectations and we do this by pro-actively *Thinking, Feeling and Behaving* in new ways that reflect our *New Authentic Self* and our *New Positive Self-Image*. Through *Intensity and Repetition*, these new thoughts, feelings and behaviours will become fully grooved in our brain to create a new set of Beliefs and Expectations in line with our aspirations. We will then perceive ourselves and the world around us in new ways and respond accordingly.

Sharon Begley in *The Plastic Mind* says: *Like sand on a beach, the brain bears the footprints of the decisions we have made, the skills we have learned, the actions we have taken. But there are also hints that mind sculpting can occur with no input from the outside world. That is, the brain can change as a result of the thoughts we have thought.*

New Autopilots

When we successfully re-program our *Beliefs and Expectations* our subconscious will from then on feed us the appropriate thoughts, feelings and behaviours in support of our *New Authentic Self*. Additionally, our *Body Processes* will also work tirelessly, 24/7, in support of our new Beliefs and Expectations.

As Cordelia Fine says in *A mind of its own: Best of all, we can recruit the brain's freelance mind to use to our own advantage – as when we consciously train the "mental butler" of our unconscious mental life efficiently and effortlessly to fulfil our aspirations. With some exertion on our part, the unconscious can come to automatically respond to certain situations in a manner that is in line with our conscious wishes.*

*Using new Thoughts, Feelings & Behaviour to re-configure
our Beliefs, Expectations & Perception Filter*

Therefore any event or situation from now on triggers a
new set of Autopilot Responses

AUTHENTIC-ENERGY-IN-MOTION

Action

Affirmations and Visualizations give us the belief and the confidence to put our *Authentic Energy* out there, but however powerful they are, they are no substitute for *Action* as they don't in themselves suddenly magic up your desired future. I have met many people who tell me they have a novel inside them but unfortunately, this is where it normally stays...

We therefore need to put our *Authentic Energy- in-Motion* by taking *Action*. This *Authentic Energy* then goes out into the world and is felt by others is probably the source of those *coincidences* that just seem to happen for no good reason. This energy comes from the head, it comes from the heart, and comes from our *Behaviour and Actions* that resonates with the outside world.

Rennie: My view of a number of self-help books is that they often give the impression that simply deciding what you want is somehow sufficient for it to appear. I have always been rather dubious of the wish-for-it-and-it-just-seems-to-arrive school of thought as it didn't seem to square with my own understanding of how things work, hence my term Authentic-Energy-in-Motion (and also WOW!-Energy-in-Motion, which you will discover in Expression). I believe that Affirmations and Visualizations need effort and action to come true.

Our Authentic Self in the Now

We have a *New Positive Vision* of our *Authentic Self* which fully engages in the present moment, which means our *Authentic Energy is* constantly working its magic to establish our new sense of self in the world. It is therefore our *New Authentic Self* that is now aware and fully mindful of the present moment and thoroughly grounded in the here and now.

NEXT STEPS

In the next step, *Well-Being,* we are going to exploit our *New Authentic Self* in our main areas of life and take the first positive step towards *Personal Fulfilment.*

Review Questions

As before, the objective of these review questions is not to test your understanding but to allow you to reflect on some of the issues raised in this step and also to help you prepare for the exercises that follow.

1. *Are you being authentic?*

2. *Are you happy with who you are and with your current situation or are there some things you would like to change?*

3. *Are there some elements of you still awaiting expression?*

4. *Do you need to accept things as they are for now and forgive yourself anything?*

5. *Are you living your own agenda or following someone else's?*

Exercises

As was said in the main introduction, you certainly do not have to complete all the exercises but just try the ones that appeal to you.

ACCEPTANCE

Exercise 1 - *Acceptance & The Confession*

A large part of our Current Self was genetically driven or was downloaded during our earliest Life Experiences and therefore from factors outside of our control.

The Confession is a key part of Acceptance. It allows us to clear the decks of anything we don't like about ourselves and our life up until now that might create negative thoughts or feelings and the negative energy that goes with it.

We therefore accept our past without resistance or struggle which removes the power of any issue to hurt us now or in the future.

We should therefore now confess to ourselves any regrets, issues, problems or personal shortcomings and to forgive ourselves, realising they are in the past and will hold no further part in our future. These issues were associated with our old self, whereas our new authentic self will be a very different proposition.

In fact we can even be thankful for these past events as they have been part of a learning exercise and have led us to where we are now and created our desire to change.

Confess and forgive yourself now and then move on

DISCOVERY

Exercise 2 - *Elements of our New Authentic Self*

This is a very important exercise as we are trying to identify who you really are - your Authentic Self.

Just get yourself a big piece of paper and read through

all the questions and just write down the answers that first come to you. Don't spend time agonizing over whether it is right or not, just write what comes into your head and quickly move on to the next question. Don't worry if you think some questions seem the same, just leave them and move on.

Just start reading and writing and I will tell you what to do with the answers at the end of this exercise.

Our Likes, Dreams & Aspirations:

What are the things you like doing more than anything else?
What excites you?
What fills you with wonder?
What do you love doing?
What gives you satisfaction?
What gives you joy?
What do you dream or daydream about?
What do you aspire to being?
When are you at your very best?
What do you find yourself thinking about?
When are you in the zone or when you lose track of time?
When do you feel most alive?
When do you feel most energised?
What did you enjoy as a child?
What do you pick up or learn most easily?
What are your most exciting or memorable experiences?
When do you feel most comfortable and relaxed?
When do you feel like you are most being yourself?
What work do we like doing?
What is your ideal or perfect day?
What are your favourite hobbies?

What do you read about or watch on television?
What kind of films do you go and see?
What kind of stories or news articles inspire you?
What kind of documentaries do you like to watch?
What kind of sports are you interested in?
What kind of friends have you got?
Where would you like to go on holiday?
What do you like to do whilst on holiday?
What do you look for in a partner?

Is there any pattern to these answers?

Our Heroes:

What people do you admire?
What qualities do you admire in other people?
What kind of people do you like to be around?
Who are your heroes?
What do your heroes do that excites or inspires you?
If you could be someone else, who would it be?
What myths or legends inspire you?
What tales of adventure or discovery inspire you?
What historical figures do you like to read about?
Is there any pattern to these answers?

What do others like about us:

How do people usually describe you?
What do they like about you?
What have you often been praised for?
What have you won prizes for?
What kind of help or advice is sought from you?
Why do people like being your friend?
What have your partners most liked about you?

ANALYSIS

OK, hopefully you should have a lot of stuff to look at and ponder over.

Did you notice any patterns to your answers? Are there some clear messages that emerged? If not keep reading your answers and pondering until a pattern emerges and you begin to understand what your main Key Attributes, Values, Motivations and Aspirations are and list your top 6

Exercise 3 – VIA Survey of Character Strengths

Once you have poured over the results of the last exercise, I would recommend you take the above test which is online. Go to: www.authentichappiness.sas.upenn.edu/ testcenter and then register for the test centre.

There are many other surveys here and I suggest you take as many as you like (I've done them all)

Any similarities or differences with your results from Exercise 2?

Exercise 4:

What elements of our emerged personal characteristics do you want to enhance and which do you want to diminish?

Exercise 5 – Completing a Self-Profile

1. *Using the information from Exercise 2, 3 & 4 confirm your top six Key Attributes, Essential Values, Motivations and Aspirations.*

2. *How would you summarise what you have found?*

3. *Describe yourself in a nutshell*

P.S. When you are being these things you are being your Authentic Self!

4. By the way, make a note of your bottom five attributes for future reference

Exercise 6 - Create an Affirmation

We can now turn our Key Attributes, Essential Values, Motivations and Aspirations into affirmations.

Affirmations can be said at any time, but they must be said with belief and feeling as it is the feeling they create that is my important than the words.

Create an affirmation that describes your Authentic Self

e.g. I am original, creative and playful
e.g. I am caring, kind and considerate
e.g. I am loyal, fair and trustworthy

Exercise 7 - Creating a Mandala

A Mandala is a personal design or symbol that usually has a concentric structure representing unity or harmony or order.

We can use this symbol as an object of meditation or as a way to associate our New Authentic Self with our Key Attributes, Essential Values, Motivations and Asprations.

This is mine for reference:

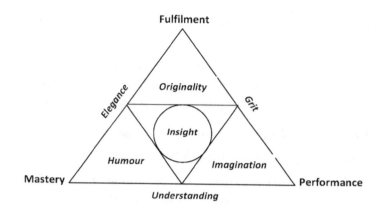

Does a Mandala come to mind?

Exercise 8 – Visualizing a New Positive Self-Image (I)

We can now take the profile of our new Authentic Self and our affirmations and use the important change tool of intensity to create a visualization of ourselves incorporating all of these new attributes and essential values.

Visualizations are probably more important than affirmations as they create a greater intensity of feeling which is exactly what we are trying to create.

1. So, put your new self-profile in front of you, together with your mandala if you have one, and really look at them, paying very close attention to every word and turning them over in your mind as if you were meditating on them.

2. Then close your eyes and in your mind's eye, see an image of yourself looking confident, totally at ease and smiling, knowing that this image now reflects your authentic self with all your Key Attributes, Essential Values, Motivations and Aspirations.

3. *Now stop thinking about it and see a blank screen in your mind's eye instead.*

4. *Keep doing this until it feels natural and your new self-image comes readily to mind. You may even find yourself laughing as you feel this technique working.*

Exercise 9 – Visualizing a new Self-Image (II)

Alternatively, you can try the following technique

5. *In your mind's eye, think of an old image of yourself before you discovered your new attributes*

6. *Now create a new self-image of your authentic self, complete with all of your Key Attributes, Essential Values, Motivations and Aspirations. You can see yourself smiling, confident and totally at ease with the world. Really luxuriate in this image and let it wash through you and over you.*

7. *Now let this image of your new authentic self get smaller and smaller until all that is left of it is a small sparkling dot that hovers just in front of you.*

8. *Now break your concentration for a second or two by thinking of something else*

9. *Now bring back your first image back into your mind's eye of your previous self and place the small sparkling dot of your new image right in the middle and let this new sparkling dot get larger and larger until it completely overwhelms your first image*

10. *Now break your concentration again and think of something different*

11. *Continue this exercise until you think it is complete*

Exercise: 10 - Direct Instruction

You can directly instruct your subconscious to accept your New Authentic Self together with your Key Attributes, Essential Values, Motivations and Aspirations. Just tell it what you want and expect. Be firm but reasonable.

In fact you can try Exercises 7, 8 & 9 and see which works best for you.

BEING AUTHENTIC

Exercise 11 - Authentic Self in the Present Moment

We want to be aware and we want to fully engage with the present moment, but we now know who it is who is should be being aware and fully engaging don't we? Yes, it's our New Authentic Self!

- We want our Authentic Self to be aware

- We want our Authentic Self to fully engage with every moment

- We want our Authentic Self to put our Authentic Energy-in-Motion

From now on, when you practice awareness, mindfulness, meditation or anything at all, it is your Authentic Self with your Authentic Energy that is doing all these things. This is the new you. Luxuriate in this, and from now on, let this feeling wash through you and over you in everything you do.

WELL-BEING

7 Steps to Self-Awareness & Personal Fulfilment

Self-Awareness	Steps	Personal Fulfilment
	GRATITUDE *Now Give Back*	
	FULFILMENT *Make it Happen*	
	EXPRESSION *Release your WOW*	
	WELL-BEING *Now Flourish!*	
	AUTHENTICITY *Become the Real You*	
	AWARENESS *Control your Mind*	
	INSIGHT *What you should know*	

Introduction

Up until now, we have been concerned with Self-Awareness and in knowing who we are but now in Well-Being, we are taking the first Step towards Personal Fulfilment, by putting our authentic selves into action – putting our Authentic Energy into our main areas of life

Many of the elements in this step draw on the on the findings of Positive Psychology which in departing from the so-called disease model of traditional psychology began to focus our attention on identifying what makes people authentic, happy and fulfilled – to flourish!

Therefore, authenticity, happiness and fulfilment have a scientific foundation to provide a series of prescriptions to create a sense of well-being. So yes, there really is a formula that can be applied to happiness and fulfilment and we will follow this formula in this step.

Achieving a sense of Well-Being is therefore a very good place to be and could be the end of the journey for some, whereas for others, it will provide a platform for even further progress towards their ultimate Personal Fulfilment.

You will not be surprised to learn that many of the fundamental elements of well-being are based around Authenticity but supported by other elements that taken together provide a positive personal infrastructure.

Authenticity in Life

Authentic Energy-in-Motion

We have identified our *New Authentic Self* and are now clear about our *Key Attributes and Essential Values*, together with our *Fundamental Motivations and Aspirations* and it is this new authentic self that is now fully engaging in the present moment. However, we are now going to go further by exploiting our *New Authentic Self* in our *Main Areas of Life*.

We have endless opportunities to be authentic by applying any one of our Attributes, Values, Motivations and Aspirations in any one of our current life areas, or even applying a combination of them to different life areas. Irrespective of how happy and fulfilled we might feel now, just imagine the difference we could feel if we were totally comfortable in our own skin and fully exploiting our authenticity in all areas of life?

If for example *Caring* and *Nurturing* are among our key attributes, the question is, which areas of life can we exploit these essential aspects of ourselves to create an even greater sense of happiness and fulfilment? Alternatively, if one of our key attributes is *Creativity*, we should examine our main areas of life to identify where we could exploit this authentic aspect of ourselves. In the exercises that follow, you will be invited to identify where you would most like to exploit aspects of your new authentic self to make the biggest differences to your life.

In *Conversations with God*, Neale Donald Walsch says: *You can know yourself to be creative or to be funny, but unless you do something that displays creativity or humour, you have nothing but a concept. It is your souls only desire to turn its grandest concept about itself into its greatest experience.*

Making the Change

When we have decided which area of our life we want to exploit our key attributes and essential values, we can use all the tools at our disposal: *Affirmations, Visualizations* and *Direct Instruction*, to make these changes happen. Incidentally, the first picture that comes to mind of ourselves being more authentic in life is often a good indication of the area where we should start as it might represent an important message from our subconscious.

We will explore this process in detail in the exercises, but in essence we are now going to:

Visualize the Positive Self Image of our New Authentic Self exploiting our Key Attributes and Essential Values in our Main Areas of Life.

We can then do in reality what we saw ourselves doing in our visualization, by taking those important first few steps with a new sense of belief and confidence, that will put our intentions into action.

The following exercise can be found at the end of this step but it is also shown below to give you a better idea of what we are trying to achieve.

1. *Generate your new Positive Self Image of you containing all your Key Attributes and Essential Values*

2. *What main life area comes first into your mind of you exploiting your new Authentic Self?*

3. *Really enjoy the vision or the movie of what you are doing and how it makes you feel (You can add any other personal qualities or attributes to this vision of you if you like)*

4. *In this vision or movie of yourself, see what you actually did in this life area to make this happen, particularly those first few steps*

5. *Now set what you visualized as your overall objective to aim for*

6. *And take Action by taking these first steps and by putting your Authentic Energy-in-Motion!*

Meaning & Direction

Being Authentic and putting our Authentic Energy-in-Motion in our main areas of life leads to a greater sense of Meaning and Direction, which together with the associated feelings of self-worth are fundamental to our sense of well-being, without which all the other supporting elements have limited value.

Knowing who we are and where we are going are therefore the essence of authenticity and the catalyst for a heightened sense of engagement, greater levels of accomplishment, more positive emotions, more authentic relationships and greater levels of optimism, vitality and resilience. In *Expression* and *Fulfilment*, we will build on our sense of meaning and direction by stretching our authenticity still further in pursuit of our *WOWS* and *Life Goals*.

Georgia: *I used to feel silly telling people (I would only tell some people) that my drive in life was to make a difference, to one person or a million, but to make a difference. I don't feel embarrassed anymore because I am proud of my driver, but also have that inner belief and knowing that I am honest and pure in my intention and so it doesn't matter to me how others perceive what I say because it is not about them, it is about me.*

And what surprised me more than anything, was once I decided upon this, I no longer felt this concern for other people's opinions, but I also strangely felt automatically like I was more credible because I wasn't waiting on their acceptance or approval. And thus, people picked up on that and believed me to be sincere. Sincerity is important to me.

Plans or Action?

I am all for setting objectives and making plans, and there are those who might want to make detailed plans for each of their life areas at this stage. This planning function will also help balance our brain by stimulating its *Left-Side* to keep us more calm and relaxed, which probably explains why it is beneficial to make *to-do* lists or to commit plans to paper.

However, I think it is equally OK if we don't move into detailed planning too early, as it might not be immediately clear what these plans should look like and anyway, having objectives and plans is no substitute for taking action, as it is these first steps that are probably the most important part of the whole exercise.

I am reminded of my good friend who during his university finals made endless revision plans but never actually did any revision. *You see Frank, I told you I would get you into this book somehow...* Therefore, in the same way that small businesses know *profit* is great but it's *cash* that's king, we could say that *plans* are great but it's *action* that's king.

We therefore need to remember that a nurturer, *nurtures* and a writer, *writes* which probably means that we should *just do it!'*

Achievement

Additionally, our need for achievements and accomplishments is also satisfied by exploiting our sense of purpose, but also provides confirmation that we are doing the right things.

As Robin Sharma said in *The Monk Who Sold His Ferrari: The real source of happiness can be stated in one word: Achievement. Lasting happiness comes from steadily working to accomplish your goals and advancing confidently in the direction of your life's purpose.*

We should therefore acknowledge each positive step we take along the way and celebrate any progress we make in moving towards our objectives. This will further strengthen our belief in our authenticity and further groove our new way of thinking and behaving in our brain to create a self-perpetuating cycle of positivity.

Rennie: I remember reading somewhere that a writer is only a writer if they actually write and so I started to follow my key attributes and interests as much as possible and apply them in my various areas of life, so not only would I know my Authentic Self, but I would also become my authentic self.

Challenging the Myths – Flicking a switch?

There are those that believe we can simply re-configure our brain to make major changes to ourselves and to our behaviour as easily as just flicking a switch on our computer. In many ways, our brain is very similar to a computer, but in some important ways it is very different.

To remove an old or existing programme on our computer, we simply find where it is located and press the delete button. We then download a new programme and apart from maybe having to restart our computer, hey presto, it's all done in a matter of minutes.

However, we have discovered that our brain works very differently. Firstly our existing programmes which are a mashup of our genetic blueprint and life experiences, are scattered all over the place and cannot therefore be found in just one location.

Secondly, during the course of time and use, these scattered bits of programming have carved deep grooves in the very grey matter of our brain and therefore to believe these old programmes can be easily located and quickly deleted just doesn't make sense. Additionally, to expect new programmes to be downloaded, installed and then to run perfectly first time, just doesn't square with our understanding of how our brain actually works.

Instant Success?

Should we really expect to change our habits of a life-time by just thinking new thoughts for just a few minutes? Do we really expect to change from a 28 handicap hacker to a major-title winning golfer in a matter of minutes without thousands of hours of practice to groove these new behaviours?

Could we really expect to become confident public speakers by doing just a few minutes of positive visualisation? I'm sure this is not the good news you were hoping for and probably explains the popularity of those books that proclaim *Instant Change, without the Effort!* I have always been suspicious of such claims and I suspect that deep down you probably feel the same way?

As Carol Dwek says in her book *Mindset: Change isn't like surgery. Even when you change, the old beliefs aren't just removed like a worn-out hip or knee and replaced with better ones. Instead, the new beliefs take their place alongside the older ones, and as they become stronger, they give you a different way to think, feel and act.*

Action, Action, Action

We know that changing our *Beliefs and Expectations* is necessary to enlist all parts of our brain and body to work tirelessly on our behalf and to keep us going in the right direction. Although this is a good start, this is not sufficient on its own, as it is the effect that these changes make to our *Intentions* and ultimately on our *Actions* that are the crucial factors that release our *Authentic Energy* into the world that makes things happen.

This is probably the real mechanism for change and no amount of wishful thinking can ever compensate for this. Lasting change will require considerable effort over a period of time using all the intensity and repetition we can muster.

Positive Engagement

Mindful deliberation and Savouring

In *Awareness*, we talked about controlling our mind and deciding whether to fully engage with our thoughts, feelings and experiences or whether we want to distance ourselves from them. *Positive Engagement* is about the former state of mind and choosing to be there in the moment and about giving whatever you are doing your full attention.

This is of course the same as being *Mindful,* which is an aspect of meditation concerned with focusing our attention on everyday events to extract their full value.

Positive Engagement and Mindfulness are therefore about slowing down and savouring every moment by concentrating on the experience in every detail, such as really tasting our food rather than just bolting it down or in really taking in the scenery rather than just drifting through the landscape without paying attention.

Flow

Flow is a consequence of putting our *Authentic Energy-in-Motion* and is the state of mind we experience when we are totally absorbed in something that fully engages our attention and focus.

It is when we are in *The Zone* or in the moment and is therefore associated with doing those activities that allow us to be ourselves and to fully exploit our unique attributes and capabilities. This is when a writer writes, when a nurturer nurtures or when an adventurer adventures. It is a state that comes from doing what we love to be doing.

As Mihaly Csikszentmihalyi says in *Flow: When people ponder further about what makes their lives rewarding, they tend to move beyond pleasant memories and begin to remember other events, that overlap with pleasurable ones, but fall into a category that is different.*

Our Authentic Self when fully engaged in the present moment and fully experiencing an authentic life is surely the principal source of joy and vitality. Joy is therefore generated by our peak experiences, when we are experiencing those things that allow us to be fully ourselves, whatever they are. As we discussed in *Insight*, perhaps we are really just *Joy Machines* in search of fulfilment?

A Sense of Control

A feeling that we are in control of ourselves and of events enhances our well-being, because to be in control implies we are fully engaged in the present moment and giving it our full attention.

On a negative note, there is evidence to suggest that those who suffer from anorexia are using the control of their food intake as a means to regain a sense of control over their lives, but on a more positive note, *Mindfulness, Flow, Deliberation* and *Savouring* all contribute to our feelings of control and therefore can positively affect our well-being.

Positive Emotions

Gratitude

Gratitude is also a key element of *Well-Being* which we are going to look in detail in our final step, but as a taster for what is to come, we might want to feel a sense of gratitude for who we are, for all the positive aspects of our life and for what we have already achieved.

We might also want to consider making *Spontaneous Acts of Kindness*. This is where we make an act of kindness, however small, often to a complete stranger and then delighting in their response. Needless to say that gratitude and kindness not only help others but they are also found to contribute to our own sense of well-being. Just remember the joy of giving gifts and seeing the recipient's response, which in most people's experience is at least as positive as actually receiving a gift themselves.

Doing things we like

We should ensure we continue to do those things that make us happy. You might think this is a blindingly obvious statement, but it is often true that we only make time for those things we feel we ought to do rather than make time for those things we like to do.

For all kinds of reasons that are usually related to the pressures of life, we can lose touch with those things that we love to do, whether it is going to the cinema, going for walks, riding our bike, making things, reading for pleasure, playing sport or going out with friends. Such things are very important in making a positive contribution to our well-being and we should therefore make a special effort to include them in our weekly routines.

Additionally, we must sometimes do those things we don't like doing and for me, it's doing my accounts and paying bills, but research has suggested that in these situations, we should focus on any positive aspects of the task or to remind ourselves how good we will feel when we get these things out of the way. Furthermore, if we expose ourselves gently to those things we don't like doing and begin to overcome any fears or anxieties, these negative feelings will dissipate over time.

Positive Memories

Having a store of *Positive Memories* is also very important for our sense of *Well-Being*. These can be memories of special times, special experiences, special places or special people, but what they have in common is that they give us a *go-to* place for our mind to re-experience those original emotions of happiness that we first experienced.

These positive memories are very useful for helping us maintain a positive frame of mind or for quickly restoring our state of well-being when we are feeling low. We should therefore make a special effort to create a list of all our positive memories to counteract our natural tendency to emphasise the negative rather than the positive.

Georgia: *I have special physical places that I visit when I need some me time, and it makes such a huge difference to me. Sleep is also my thing. If I don't get enough sleep it deeply affects me.*

Neutralizing Negative Thoughts

We discussed this topic in *Awareness*, but it is also relevant here. We have learned how to control our mind in such a way that we don't ignore negative thoughts or feelings, but neither do we allow ourselves to be taken over by them, but instead, we hold them in awareness where they can do no harm and where they will eventually pass like clouds in the sky.

Previous Accomplishments

A previous accomplishment can be anything that took a major effort to complete or can be anything that we are particularly proud of.

It could also be anything that we have learned or achieved which could include winning an award, gaining a promotion, or achieving a qualification.

It could also be a sustained period of time we devoted to a particular project or something we dedicated a large proportion of our lives towards, such as raising a family or caring for someone. It can also be the result of dealing successfully with any challenging or troubling situation that we had to face. All of these activities or events gave us satisfaction at the time but they also provide positive memories to give us satisfaction in the future and a renewed sense of well-being.

Confidence, Optimism & Hope

No matter what has happened in the past, our *Authentic Self* and *Authentic Energy* is now moving us in the right direction.

Being *Authentic* may not always be easy as it might require us to unravel certain aspects of our life before we can move forward which can make us feel as if we are taking two steps backwards before taking one step forwards. Furthermore, not everything will go to plan and we are likely to have down days as well as up days.

However, we should remain convinced that as we are doing the right things, the right things will happen, which is very different from just wishful thinking and sitting around waiting for things to happen.

We are now taking those positive actions in all areas of life that reflect our authentic selves and given that many of our psychological issues can be traced back to the C *word* – *Confidence*, this positive philosophy should provide us with a realistic sense of confidence, optimism and hope for the future.

Just Smile!

It might sound a bit silly, but our neuroscience friends have found that smiling has a positive effect on our brain and on our mood to make us feel happier.

The very act of pulling our mouth into a smile activates specific circuits in our brain and releases certain chemicals that heighten our mood.

This is an aspect of the *Mind-Body Link* we discussed in *Insight* and of what psychologists call *Behavioural*

Activation, where the very act of forcing ourselves to do something we don't like or think we can't do, actually increases our chances of being able to do it more easily in the future.

Positive Relationships

Love & Social Bonding

We are social animals who like spending time with others. Not only is this enjoyable in itself but it has been found that those with close bonds and positive relationships with others have increased levels of Well-Being and live healthier and happier lives. We appear to have specific circuits in our brain that respond to these relationships by releasing hormones that lift our mood and enhance our physical well-being.

Is love the highest form of human expression? Were Lennon & McCartney right when they said that all we need is love? I guess we have had to experience love to answer these questions as love does not lend itself to easy description, although the power of love seems to have created some of the most beautiful physical manifestations in our world.

Spending time with significant others is something that can get lost in the hurly burly of normal life and we should therefore make a special effort to keep these important relationships going. And we are not just talking about human bonds, as close attachments with our pets are likely to be equally beneficial.

People with Positive Energy

Energy is infectious and we should therefore look to spend more time with people with positive energy: Those who are optimistic, those who want to try new things or explore new ideas and those who like who we are and encourage us to be ourselves.

If we are looking to share our goals and plans and ideas with someone else, then these are the people we should confide in as we will also benefit from their own positive energy.

We should however be wary of sharing too much, too early, with those who are less positive as the last thing we want is to become discouraged at such an early stage.

Collaborating with others who share our interests and goals is another positive aspect of bonding.

There is probably a group close to you where you can share your interest in music, photography, creative writing, rock-climbing or whatever.

Not only would such people provide a supportive and encouraging environment, but they might also be able to provide complimentary talents and resources to help us progress our goals. We might also find some allies or supporters who could provide significant help.

Give & Take

We must give to our relationships before we expect to receive from them in return.

This give and take attitude to social bonding is therefore very important, but so is the quality of this giving.

As we discussed in *Mindfulness*, the giving of your full attention and interest to someone by really listening and responding to what they are saying is an important part of rapport and an important contributor to positive relationships.

Asking a significant other to recount their day and then to ask to ask further questions to clarify certain points or to explore issues still further can be very powerful. Listen carefully each time that someone you care about tells you about something good that happened to them. Go out of your way to respond actively and constructively, ask them to relive the event and spend lots of time responding.

Positive Infrastructure

Exercise

There is a very strong link between exercise and *Well-Being*. Not only does exercise help our general health, particularly our cardiovascular fitness, but it also makes us feel even better about how we feel and about how we look, which is of course a positive thing in itself and the feeling you get from fitting into those old trousers or in being able to wear that favourite old dress should of course not be underestimated.

But in order to get the best out of any activity, even exercise, we must perform it Mindfully, that is we must give whatever we are doing our full attention in order to receive its full benefit. Even just stretching has a very positive effect, particularly as part of a mindfulness exercise, although any kind of exercise is equally beneficial, particularly low impact exercise for those of us who might not have been as active as we should have been lately.

Swimming and walking, particularly fast walking, are excellent exercises, so what are you waiting for, just put on your trainers or swimwear and get out there!

Sleep & Nutrition

I'm beginning to feel like I'm teaching a grandmother how to suck eggs here, but these elements are all important as part of the *Positive Infrastructure* that support our sense of well-being. Good sleep and good nutrition are therefore important factors and should not be underestimated.

Rennie: I have found that cutting down on carbohydrates does wonders for my weight and energy levels and secondly I have ceased to fight my natural sleep patterns. I prefer to stay up late and get up late, which means that I live at the wrong end of the clock from most people.

But rather than go to bed too early and lie awake for hours or wake up early still feeling tired, I have learned to listen to my own body and adapt my sleep patterns accordingly, even though this puts me totally out of synch with almost everyone else, including my wife! Perhaps this is just another aspect of being authentic?

Sunshine & Nature

Getting some sunshine on your face or body does wonders for our spirit. This is not to say we should go mad and turn ourselves into lobsters at every opportunity, but it is a proven fact that as a source of vitamin D, sunshine is essential for our well-being.

Even when the sun isn't shining, just getting ourselves into the fresh air and enjoying the simple majesty of nature makes a positive contribution to our sense of well-being.

Resilience

Bouncing Back

Resilience is a very important aspect of *Positive Psychology* and is a major contributor to our continuing sense of *Well-Being*. Things will not always go to plan and we should expect to have tough times and set-backs along the way, because if we didn't experience bad times, we wouldn't know what good times felt like.

As with many of our *Essential Characteristics*, there is a strong *Genetic Component* to *Resilience* which means that some people are just more naturally resilient than others. But, everybody has the capability to develop this aspect of their personality by learning how to push their resilience towards the upper end of their own *Genetic Set-Range*.

Knowing who we are and being authentic in the main areas of our lives has now given us a solid platform from which to withstand set-backs and difficulties and to weather these storms until they inevitably pass.

This is what *Resilience* is all about, we can't control what will happen but we can control how we respond and how we deal with it. It is this ability to *bounce-back* that typifies *Resilience*.

Stuart: *I have a problem with resilience which is probably due to my inability to control my own thoughts and the fact that they can go negative to spiral out of control.*

The Elements of Resilience

We have been discussing all the elements of resilience throughout this step, but it might be useful to bring all these elements together now.

A sense of purpose and direction in life

The confidence, vitality and optimism that comes from authenticity

Accomplishments and achievements

A positive store of memories and experiences

Our ability to neutralize negative thoughts and feelings

Our ability to fully engage with our experiences to savour every moment

Our willingness to do what makes us happy

Having a network of positive, supportive and collaborative relationships

Having a supportive infrastructure of positive activities, exercise, nutrition, sleep, sunshine

Having a sense of optimism and belief about the future

In the final analysis however, having a clear sense of self and the confidence to be ourselves will provide us with the continued motivation to put our authentic energy in motion to create the life we want and to help us to bounce back from the inevitable difficulties and problems we all face and help us to *just deal with it.*

As Martin Seligman says in *Flourish: So one thing that clinical psychology needs to develop in light of the heritable stubbornness of human pathologies is a psychology of "dealing with it". We need to tell our patients, "Look, the truth is that many days – no matter how successful we are in therapy – you will wake up feeling blue and thinking that life is hopeless. Your job as a patient is not only to fight these feelings but also to live heroically: functioning well, even when you are sad.*

The Essential Life Balance

It is clear that we can develop our resilience by enhancing any aspect of *Well-Being* and it might not take much to swing the essential life balance in our favour. It is easy to feel that the world is against us or we are struggling against the tide, finding it difficult to impose ourselves on external events and might therefore feel that our current life balance feels like this:

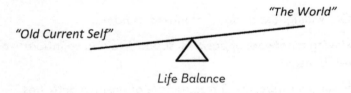

"The World"

"Old Current Self"

Life Balance

✖ *Little knowledge of our authentic self / Lacking purpose and direction*

✖ *Inwardly focused / Not fully engaging in life's experiences*

✖ *Negative thoughts and feelings*

✖ *Acting on autopilot*

✖ *Lacking in energy and vitality*

✖ *Anxious / Fearful / Frustrated*

✖ *Few positive emotions, positive relationships, positive infrastructure*

✖ *Less resilience, confidence, hope and optimism*

But by learning how to control our awareness and to better focus it on more positive thoughts and feelings, by becoming more *Authentic* in all of our areas of life and incorporating the elements of *Well-Being* into our life, we should become more *Resilient* and tip our *Life Balance* in our favour:

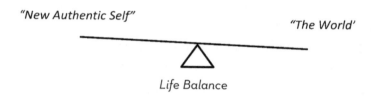

"New Authentic Self"

"The World'

Life Balance

✔ *Knowledge of our authentic self, key attributes, values, motivations and aspirations*

✔ *Greater sense of purpose and direction*

✔ *More positive engagement in life / More energetic and vital*

✔ *Better control of awareness, thoughts, feelings and actions*

✔ *Less use of autopilot programmes*

✔ *Putting our energy in motion in key life areas*

✔ *Totally engaging and experiencing life*

✔ *More positive emotions, positive relationships, positive infrastructure*

✔ *Greater resilience, confidence, hope and optimism*

Review Questions

The objective of these review questions is not to test your understanding but to allow you to reflect on some of the issues raised in this step and also to help you prepare for the exercises that follow.

1. *Are you good at celebrating your successes?*

2. *In which areas of your life could you be more your authentic self?*

3. *Are you making the time to still do what you enjoy doing and looking after yourself properly?*

4. *Are you giving enough of yourself to your most important relationships?*

5. *How resilient are you?*

Exercises

As was said in the main introduction, you certainly do not have to complete all the exercises but just try the ones that appeal to you.

Exercise 1 – Exploiting our New Authentic Self in Main Life Areas (I)

We are going to exploit our Key Attributes, Essential Values, Motivations and Aspirations in our current areas of life.

Using the table below, I would like you to think about and then rate your current satisfaction with each of your current areas of your life.

Life Area	Current Score 1-10	Which Key Attribute or Essential Value would help you improve your score?
Engagement		
Resilience		
Energy & Vitality		
Motivation		
Kindness		
Fun		
Health or Fitness		
Joy		
Achievement		
Authenticity		
Personal Development		
Satisfaction		
Relationships		
Finances		
Work / Career		
Family		

1. Generate your new Positive Self Image of you containing all your Key Attributes and Essential Values

2. Looking at the table above, what Life Area and Key Attribute/ Essential Value/Motivation or Aspiration do you feel you should start with first?

3. See yourself in this life area making a real difference with this selected element and really enjoy the vision or the movie of what you are doing and how it makes you feel (You can add any other personal qualities or attributes to this vision of you if you like)

4. In this vision or movie of yourself, see what you actually did in this life area to make this happen, particularly those first few steps

5. Now set what you visualized as your overall objective to aim for

6. And take Action by taking these first steps and by putting your Authentic Energy-in-Motion!

It's probably best not to overload yourself with too many activities at this stage, probably two or three is the maximum, but there are no fixed rules for this as it depends on what you feel comfortable with.

When you feel ready, move on to another area or attribute.

Exercise 2 – Exploiting Key Attributes & Essential Values in Main Life Areas (II)

This is an alternative exercise to the one above that adopts a less structured approach that might appeal more to some people

1. Generate your new Positive Self Image of you containing all your Key Attributes and Essential Values

2. What main life area comes first into your mind of you exploiting your new Authentic Self?

3. Really enjoy the vision or the movie of what you are doing and how it makes you feel (You can add any other personal qualities or attributes to this vision of you if you like)

4. In this vision or movie of yourself, see what you actually did in this life area to make this happen, particularly those first few steps

5. Now set what you visualized as your overall objective
    to aim for

6. And take Action by taking these first steps and by
    putting your Authentic Energy-in-Motion!

Exercise 3 – Positive Emotions

We are going to create a positive store of emotions,
memories, learning and accomplishments that you can go
back to at any time in order to lift your mood.

It can be a special place, time or memory where you
were particularly safe, content or happy or it can also be
when you did something special or when you achieved
something you are particularly proud of. Make a list of all
these times and places and practice going back to each
one in your mind to re-live the event in every detail, really
luxuriate in the experience and live it again as if it was
really happening now.

You can now tap into any of these experiences whenever
you like and they will transform your mood.

Exercise 4 – Neutralising negative thoughts or feelings

In this exercise, we are going to hold any negative thoughts
and feelings in our awareness and just let them pass. So if
we become aware of any negative thoughts or feelings at
any time in the day or during any of the other mindfulness
exercises outlined below, we should do the following:

1. Allow any negative thought or feeling to arise
    whenever.

2. Don't try to ignore it or fight it, but just acknowledge
    what it is and even say to yourself, "Ha! It's that silly old

thought again!" And give yourself a little smile, while holding it in your awareness ever so gently.

3. *Wait for it to pass and then return to whatever else you were doing.*

4. *Keep doing this as and when necessary*

By the way, you shouldn't be discouraged about having to do this often as it means you are exercising awareness and control.

Exercise 5 – Positive Relationships

1. Identify your most important relationships

2. Decide on one action that would strengthen this relationship further

3. Take that action

Exercise 6 – Special Activities

For all kinds of different reasons, we sometimes forget to do those things we like doing best and end up only doing those things we must do.

1. *Take a few minutes to list all of those activities you like doing or used to like doing before you got busy, such as walking, playing sport, reading, going out with friends, going to the cinema or art galleries etc.*

2. *Now pick two of these activities and plan to do them in the current week, no excuses accepted.*

Exercise 7 – Positive aspects of Negative Tasks

When you are next faced with doing something you really dislike doing, focus on a positive aspect of the task you do like or on the good feeling you will get when the task is done.

1. *Think of the task you really dislike but have to do*

2. *Make a list of all the positive aspects of this task*

3. *Focus on these positives when doing the task*

Exercise 8 – Being in control

This is an exercise that I find that produces incredible feelings of self-control and positivity.

1. *Just stop doing one thing that you want to cut out, whether it's watching television before 9pm or eating biscuits in the day and try it for 2 days initially.*

2. *Every time you have the urge to do what you have decided against, resist it!*

3. *How does this make you feel?*

Exercise 9 – Just get out there!

We talked about looking after yourself in the main text of this step and of course it's all very obvious stuff, so obvious we don't often do those things for some reason.

So to give you a good kick-start, I want you to pull on your trainers and go for a 30 minute fast walk every day for the next 7 days.

How does this make you feel?

Exercise 10 – Rescue Remedy

This can be used at any time when you feel anxious or stressed or just a bit down and should put you back where you would rather be.

1. *Just take some time out and take some deep breaths*

2. *Focus your eyes on something and really concentrate, such as on a nearby object or even on the back of your hands. Really look at the object to really take it in*

3. *When you are feeling calm, visualize a positive memory or your Mandala or your positive self-image or a vision of you being authentic in an area of life or of you achieving your WOW! – whatever feels best for you and really re-create all the emotions of this visualization and stay with this visualisation for as long as you want to.*

4. *Now clear your mind of everything and take a few deep breaths. You should feel calmer as a result.*

EXPRESSION

7 Steps to Self-Awareness & Personal Fulfilment

	GRATITUDE *Now Give Back*	Personal Fulfilment ↑
	FULFILMENT *Make it Happen*	
	EXPRESSION *Release your WOW*	
	WELL-BEING *Now Flourish!*	
Self-Awareness ↑	**AUTHENTICITY** *Become the Real You*	
	AWARENESS *Control your Mind*	
	INSIGHT *What you should know*	

Introduction

In Authenticity and Well-Being, we moved from Self-Awareness to the first part of Personal Fulfilment by exploiting our Authentic Self in our main areas of life. In Expression, we move into the second part of Personal-Fulfilment by pushing our Authenticity to its fullest extent.

We are moving away from the relative warmth and security of base-camp and beginning the climb towards the summit of our existence and are therefore in the realms of Transformational Change, rather than making incremental changes as we have until this Step.

But, we will also discover that the journey towards Personal-Fulfilment is just as important as the destination itself as we begin to feel the excitement of our Authentic Self being galvanised by the WOWS! that come from our Life Goals and Life Purpose.

We have come a long way to get to this point and have therefore earned the right to take a shot at the big one. All the previous work we have done in Insight, Awareness, Authenticity and Well-Being will provide the launch pad for what we are going to do now.

A WOW! – an extension of Authenticity

A *WOW!* is an emotion – a positive feeling magnified to its fullest extent. It is a state of high excitement that comes from imagining the achievement of something fundamental to our existence. Our *WOWS* come from deep within and reflect who we really are; they are therefore an extension of our *Authentic Self*, when it is being fully expressed.

We have done a lot of work to get to this point in learning how our mind and brain works and in learning how to control our *Awareness*. In *Authenticity* we identified our *Key Attributes and Essential Values* – effectively the essence that makes us who we are – and then in *Well-Being*, developed the notion of *Authenticity* still further by exploiting these *Key Attributes and Essential Values* in our main areas of life to achieve the first part of our *Personal Fulfilment*.

Still something missing?

Even after being authentic in your main life areas, do you feel there is something important still left undone? Is there something in your mind that won't seem to go away that stops you feeling totally comfortable with who you are and what you are doing? Perhaps you have a completely audacious or unreasonable dream that just won't go away that keeps gnawing away at you?

Pursuing our authenticity in the key areas of life should have created a greater sense of meaning and purpose and provided us with some important clues about what we should be doing with our life. But we are now going much further and pushing our authenticity to its limits of expression – to think the unthinkable, to throw our natural caution to the wind, to make a leap of faith and to push our boundaries way beyond our *Comfort Zone*. We might therefore have to take risks we would normally not even consider and do things we would usually be too scared to do. Welcome to the realms of *Transformational Change*.

Continuing the Journey

As we discussed in *Well-Being*, being your authentic self in all areas of life, whilst also being fully engaged in the present moment, should be personally fulfilling and could therefore be a good place to end your journey. However, for some of us, this will not be enough and if it's any consolation, I know exactly how this feels. You should therefore feel entirely justified in going no further and taking your winnings home without placing any further bets.

The following steps of *Fulfilment* and *Gratitude* are still relevant and you can go straight to these Steps now. However, if you want to make further progress towards your ultimate *Personal Fulfilment* in pursuit of your *Life*

Goals and Life Purpose, you must be prepared to *Release Your WOW!*

Audacious Goals

We might all have all felt a *WOW!* at some stage in our life, when our soul has been stirred and lifted to new heights and when our whole body radiates with excitement – when you were so passionately engaged in something that nothing else mattered. So now is the time to admit if there is still an elephant in the room? What is it called? Surely, we can finally own up to what we really have to do to achieve our ultimate personal fulfilment? Surely we have earned the right to give it a shot?

We are usually constrained by what we *believe* our abilities to be rather than being constrained by what our abilities *actually* are and therefore whatever we believe to be possible sets limits on what we will subsequently achieve. Perhaps we can now raise our sights and set *Audacious Goals*, only then will we be taken outside of our *Self-Imposed Limitations and Comfort Zone*.

Unless we push ourselves beyond our previously self-imposed limits, our true capabilities might forever remain dormant. The only way to identify the uppermost limits of those capabilities set by our genetic blueprint is to push ourselves as far as we can and to see how far this will take us.

As Robin Sharma says in *The Monk Who Sold His Ferrari*: *When you are inspired by some great purpose or some extraordinary project, all of your thoughts break their bonds: your mind transcends limitations, your consciousness expands in every direction and you find* yourself in a new, great and wonderful world. Dormant forces, faculties and talents become alive and you discover yourself to be a greater person than you ever dreamed yourself to be.

Only leap when ready

There is therefore a difficult decision to be made here. On the one hand we don't want to waste an opportunity to fulfil our life purpose, but on the other hand we don't want to take crazy risks that might jeopardize our future well-being.

I have always worried about those who encourage us to make a massive leap before we are ready, to ask us to jump into the water before we have learned to swim. I think we should be wary of being seduced by those who may already have a firm idea of their own *Key Attributes and Essential Values* and who may have already completed many of our steps before they arrived at their own jumping off point. Such people may also have a well-established support system in place that would cushion them financially, physically and emotionally.

A *WOW!* is not an incremental step, as was the case with exploiting your key attributes in *Well-Being* and therefore it seems to me that to take the ultimate step without first strengthening your existing position is just not sensible.

Trying to make the summit of Everest without first establishing a secure base camp is certainly heroic but probably not very sensible or practical. Besides, by taking a more incremental approach, you might learn many important things about yourself along the way.

Hopefully the reason why the *7-Steps* have been put

together in the way they have is now becoming clear. I didn't want you to consider such a massive step until you were fully prepared:

Until you had learned how to control your mind and its thoughts and feelings

Until you had found out who you really are

Until you had started to flex your authentic muscles in your existing areas of life

Until you had surrounded yourself with a solid infrastructure to provide essential support and resilience.

So, is this the right time for you to go for what you feel you must do? Only you can decide.

WOWS! & Life Goals

Why WOWS! are so important

A *WOW!* is the feeling you get when you think about pursuing or achieving a *Life Goal*, so why am I not cutting straight to the chase and asking you about these goals? If you will allow me to answer my own question, there are a number of reasons for this. The first is that a feeling of *WOW!* is more natural and easier to imagine than merely producing a list of goals and secondly, it is this *feeling* and strength of emotion generated by our *WOW!* that ultimately creates its own fulfilment.

By focusing on WOWS rather than on life goals, this also prevents us from becoming too obsessed with specific objectives and outcomes rather than being focused on channelling all our attention and energy into the present moment, which is an issue we will consider throughout this step and also in *Fulfilment.*

Why are WOWS! so important?

- *They allow you to fully identify the elephant in the room*
- *They are an expression of our Life Goals*
- *They come from our essential nature, from the very core of our being*
- *They are the fullest expression of our Authentic Self*
- *They are our birth-right*
- *They will further energize our engagement in the present moment*
- *We have earned the right to go for them*
- *They allow us to think big and move outside our comfort zone*
- *They will propel us towards our personal fulfilment*
- *They will bring joy, happiness and deep satisfaction*
- *They will continue to pull us in the right direction*
- *They fulfil our evolutionary inheritance*
- *They add to diversity and help develop the human species*
- *They will further re-programme our Beliefs and Intentions*
- *They will bring our Subconscious Mind even further on board with our desires*
- *They will inspire us to take the crucial first steps towards our Life Goals*

- *They will motivate us to take our energy out into the wider world to make things happen and to create a pathway to our goals*

- *They will provide continuous energy and motivation to keep us going no matter what*

- *They are an expression of our Life Purpose (See below)*

From the Heart

WOWS! are said to come from the heart, from the very core of our being. Interestingly, our heart is supposedly a much more powerful producer of electrical and magnetic energy than our brain and therefore feelings that emanate from the heart should resonate much more strongly with the outside world. Perhaps this is because heartfelt feelings are more reflective of who we are and are therefore more genuine and why change is more effective if it is heartfelt, rather than just imagined?

That is why *WOWS* are so important, as they reflect our heartfelt wishes and fill us with the passion and motivation that brings about their own fulfilment. Different *WOWS* probably create different patterns and connections in our brain and probably create different frequencies of energy vibration in the outside world. Different *WOWS* therefore create different *Thoughts, Feelings, Actions and Experiences* and if we believe in the *Law of Attraction*, they will attract different people, situations and opportunities.

Identifying your WOWS!

So, if you are still with me, you might want to consider the following questions that are also found in the exercises that follow this step.

- *What makes you go WOW! just thinking about it?*
- *What would you do if you were the only person you had to justify it to?*
- *If you could inhabit a parallel reality for a day, who would you be?*
- *Who are your heroes? Do you want to do what they do?*
- *If you could have a dream come true, what would it be?*
- *What have you always wanted but were too afraid to ask?*

I suspect that deep down you already know what your WOWS are and have probably known for some time but have kept them hidden for fear of embarrassment or because you have not wanted to be seen as unrealistic.

Rennie: My WOWS that I feel when I imagine certain things happening helped me to identify my Life Goals. These goals turned out to be all extensions of my Key Attributes and Essential Values that constitute my Authentic Self but are of course pushed as far as possible. My Life Goals are to write a strategy book based on my original techniques and framework (which is now done) to publish Release Your WOW! (now completed if you are reading this!) and finally to write a novel (currently called The Right Thing) which will hopefully be made into a film. Watch this space...

Life Purpose

Common Theme?

When we think about our *Authentic Self, Key Attributes and Essential Values, WOWS and Life Goals*, does a pattern emerge? Do they suggest a common theme? Are they linked together in some way that suggests an over-arching *Life Purpose*? Do they suggest a *Statement of Personal Intent* that just seems to summarise who we are?

This is our Life Purpose and we can create *Affirmations and Visualisations* in the same way we did for *Authenticity* to help change our *Beliefs and Expectations* and the *Thoughts, Feelings and Actions* they generate. And provided that our striving towards our Life Purpose is based on our *Authentic Self*, we can be the only judge of what this Life Purpose is. We should be wary of listening to anyone who tells us otherwise as they might only weigh us down with their own *Fears* and *Limiting Beliefs*.

Rennie: My authentic self, key attributes, essential values, WOWS and life goals all come together to suggest an overarching Life Purpose as follows: My Life Purpose is to Understand, Explain, Entertain & Inspire! Everything that I am doing now is related to this.

Aspirations v Delusions

I have often been asked to explain the difference between an *Authentic Aspiration* and a Delusion. To try and answer this question, I have devised an *Anti-Delusion Test*.

In my view, if you can answer most of these questions in the affirmative, you should take it as read that you are aspirational rather than delusional:

- *Do your Life Goals reflect your Authentic Self and your Key Attributes and Essential Values?*

- *Have your been successfully exploiting your Key Attributes and Essential Values in the various areas of your life?*

- *Have you had any previous successes in areas that are related to your Life Goals?*

- *Have other people suggested you should go after your Life Goals?*

- *Would your life remain unfulfilled if you did not strive to achieve your Life Goals?*

- *Do you often have day-dreams or visualizations of yourself doing what have to do?*

- *Have you already taken positive Action as well as had dreams and intentions?*

- *Are you prepared to make sacrifices to put in the hard work to make it happen?*

In the final analysis, the only person to decide on what is achievable versus what is delusional is you and I suspect there are more people who fail to go after their legitimate life goals than there are people who chase unrealistic dreams. I think it is better to have gone for them than to have wasted the opportunity that our inherited genes have given us – rather like being passed the baton for the next leg in the relay but then deciding not to race.

As Susan Jeffers in *Feel the Fear and Do It Anyway* says: *People who refuse to take risks live with a feeling of dread that is far more severe than what they would feel if they took the necessary risks to make them less helpless*

WOW Energy-in-motion

Our *WOWS!* help us to identify our audacious objectives or *Life Goals* which become a star in the sky that give us an aiming point to keep us moving in the right direction. Although we don't have detailed plans at this stage or precise time-scales when things should happen, these things are probably less important than putting our energy out there and actually making a start.

Our *WOW Energy* works first on ourselves by galvanizing our very being and motivating us to put our energy into *Action* in pursuit of our *Life Goals*. This energy is then released into the outside world which is the mechanism that actually makes things happen. The first steps we take towards our life goals begin the process of releasing our WOW Energy into the outside world and are therefore of crucial importance.

The fact that we have also further reconfigured our *Beliefs and Expectations* filter means that our aspirations and intentions are now working for us 24/7, even when we are not consciously thinking about them.

This is very different from just thinking about our goals and wishing for them to come true as we are making things happen ourselves by putting our *Authentic* and *WOW Energy-in-Motion*. How this makes us feel and the inner passion and motivation it creates are the principal mechanisms by which our *Life Goals* will be achieved.

Furthermore, our *Authentic* Self that fully engages with the present moment is now galvanized with this *WOW Energy-in-Motion*, surely a win-win!

Stuart: *I don't think I have enough conviction in who I*

am to put enough energy out there and as a result, the opportunities are not as forthcoming as I would like. I need to do more than to just think about what I want to happen. I need more action.

Review Questions

The objective of these review questions is not to test your understanding but to allow you to reflect on some of the issues raised in this step and also to help you prepare for the exercises that follow.

1. Which elements of your authentic self are being the easiest to exploit?

2. Which areas of your life would you like to greatly expand?

3. What elements of your authentic self might you fully express?

4. What do you often day-dream about?

5. What do you think you are here for?

Exercises

As was said in the main introduction, you certainly do not have to complete all the exercises but just try the ones that appeal to you.

WOWS! & LIFE GOALS

Exercise 1 – Identifying Your WOWS!

A WOW! is our ultimate thrill. It is what we feel when we are totally expressing our essential nature and doing what we should be doing with our life. These WOWS! reflect *our Life Goals and therefore help us tease out what these goals really are. Just consider the following:*

- *What makes you go WOW! just thinking about it?*

- *What would you do if you were the only person you had to justify it to?*

- *If you could inhabit a parallel reality for a day, who would you be?*

- *Who are your heroes? Do you want to do what they do?*

- *If you could have a dream come true, what would it be?*

- *What have you always wanted but were too afraid to ask?*

Exercise 2 – Identifying Your Life Goals

What do your WOWS imply? Is there a clear message here?

Now re-state your WOWS in terms of Life Goals.

If for example, your WOW is seeing one of your painting on display in a public gallery, presumably your Life Goal is something to do with painting?

If for example, your WOW is to see yourself helping disadvantaged young children succeeding in life, presumably your Life Goal is something to do with working with a caring organisation?

Exercise 3 – Putting our WOW! Energy-in-motion

We now want to put your WOW Energy-in-Motion by taking Action!

1. *What is the first step you could take to get your energy*

out there and to move one step nearer your goal?

2. *Take that step and see what happens...*

3. *Take another step. Can you now see a way forward?*

Exercise 4 – Time Travel Planning

Although planning is much less important at this early stage as it's more important to take the first step and to set your WOW! Energy-in-motion, we could travel backwards in time from the fulfilment of our Goal, noticing the steps we took along the way.

1. *In your mind, go forwards to the time when your goal is achieved and feel your WOW being realised. Fully engage in the experience*

2. *Now look backwards into the past and see how your goal was achieved, noticing all the steps taken, particularly the earliest ones*

3. *Take that first step*

LIFE PURPOSE

Exercise 5 – Identifying Your Life Purpose

1. *Do your Key Attributes, Essential Values, your Authentic Self and your WOWS! have anything in common? Do they suggest an over-arching purpose or a common thread that seems to link them together?*

2. *Just play around with these ideas and waste a lot of paper writing thoughts and ideas until something starts to emerge. It will.*

3. *Write a Life Purpose Statement: My Life Purpose is to...*

4. *Direct a film of yourself pursuing your Life Purpose*

and visualize yourself doing all those things you feel passionate about. Really let the feeling wash all over you, filling you with WOW! Energy

5. *Revisit your WOWS, Life Goals and Life Purpose regularly, particularly in the morning when you wake as this will groove them in your mind*

FULFILMENT

7 Steps to Self-Awareness & Personal Fulfilment

Self-Awareness ↑	**GRATITUDE** *Now Give Back*	↑ **Personal Fulfilment**
	FULFILMENT *Make it Happen*	
	EXPRESSION *Release your WOW*	
	WELL-BEING *Now Flourish!*	
	AUTHENTICITY *Become the Real You*	
	AWARENESS *Control your Mind*	
	INSIGHT *What you should know*	

Introduction

We have done most of the hard work in the previous steps of Insight, Awareness, Authenticity, Well-Being and Expression and are now in the home straight with the finishing line, representing our Personal Fulfilment, now coming into view.

We have learned how our mind controls both our perceptions and our experience and have learned how to harness its power through the control and focus of our awareness. We have also discovered who we really are and better understand the contribution that our unique capabilities can make in all areas of our life. We have then created a positive infrastructure around ourselves that gives us the best possible chance of securing an enduring sense of well-being. And finally we may have identified those things we must do to achieve the fullest extent of our personal fulfilment.

In this Step, we are concerned with realising our Life Goals and Life Purpose by releasing our WOW! Energy into the outside world that keeps us on track and guides our every move. We are aiming for the summit of our authenticity and expression but have something of a balancing act to perform. On the one hand we are trying to influence events, but on the other hand we don't want to force the issue too much for fear of losing touch with the present moment where everything happens and where all opportunities emerge.

Moving Towards our Goals

Following the Star

With *WOWS*, we are in the realms of *Transformational Change* which is very different from exploiting our authenticity in our main life areas, which is what we discussed in Well-Being.

With the changes we are considering in *Expression*, it is even more important to focus on our new beliefs and expectations and to keep putting our *WOW Energy* out there, rather than to create detailed plans and actions.

The fact is, we would probably go nuts trying to anticipate every eventuality or control every event related to our goals and likely to become disheartened when things inevitably don't happen as planned. There are simply too many variables involved which makes it unrealistic to have a complete plan with all the necessary steps clearly detailed, especially as we will probably need some unforeseen help along the way.

Additionally, if we focus too much on the future and obsess too much about specific outcomes, we will lessen our engagement with the present moment where everything actually happens. It might also be counter-productive to have rigid plans too early as this might preclude some unexpected opportunities emerging as our *WOW! Energy* makes itself felt in the outside world. We should therefore use our goals like a bright star in the sky or as a lighthouse that keeps us heading in the right direction and to illuminate our path.

Opportunities will emerge

Although we may be following our star in the sky, we cannot see over the horizon, so we cannot see our precise destination or the exact nature of the journey we will take to get there. But if we continue to follow our star, we will get there in the end and besides, we might find something interesting along the way that we didn't expect to find.

We should be assured that the next steps towards our goals will emerge as our *Authentic Self* and *WOW! Energy* generates the *Action* that in turn will create the opportunities, coincidences, and happenchance's we will need. Our *Affirmations and Visualizations* are therefore of crucial importance to create and maintain those positive feelings of *Belief and Expectation* that will keep us moving in the right direction and make our *WOWS!* and *Life Goals* happen.

John: I know deep down is that I need to get better at dealing with opportunity immediately and not after persuasion - I need to get better at identifying opportunity and seizing it

WOW in the NOW

On the one hand, we must feel our *WOWS!* with intensity and repetition, whereas on the other hand, we must be totally connected to the *NOW* where everything happens and where everything is created.

Which begs the question of how we can do both things at the same time? In short, our *WOW will energise our NOW!* Our *Authentic Self* that fully engages in the present moment will now become turbocharged by our *WOW Energy.*

Deepak Chopra in *The Seven Spiritual Laws of Success* says: *Intention is the real power behind desire. Our intention is for the future, but our attention is in the present. We must accept the present but intend the future. If we are too attached to the future, we are not grounded in the present.*

Another way of dealing with this issue is to visualize our *WOWS!* just before we go to sleep and just after we have woken up each morning, as these are the times when our mind is at its most naturally receptive. Additionally, even though we would like to be fully engaged in the present moment, we can also *Flash the Future* every now and again with a quick *Visualization* that envisions our *WOWS and Goals.* Even when we are not actually thinking about our *Authentic Self* and our *WOWS!* but are fully engaging with the present moment, these thoughts and feelings we have created are increasingly grooved in our subconscious mind and are working 24/7 to deliver on our beliefs and expectations.

The universe moves in mysterious ways...

It has often been said that *the universe moves in mysterious ways...* Putting our *WOW! Energy* out into the world is therefore not like ordering a pizza. Unlike the pizza, our goals are unlikely to be delivered within minutes to our exact recipe and exactly on time.

Having a very fixed and inflexible view about a specific outcome does not allow any wriggle room or artistic licence for what might eventually happen. The whole issue of intention is not an exact science and therefore of particular importance is to maintain the belief and expectation that our *WOW! Energy* will deliver in the end, as this will keep us focused on doing the right things in every moment. This implies we should not be too attached and fixated on the exact nature of the end result, nor should we be too prescriptive in the way this end result will come about.

It is also very difficult to tell when something is in transition, as oftentimes, nothing seems to be happening. This is especially true of the kind of changes we are trying to effect in *Expression* and it might seem that although we are putting lots of energy out there, nothing seems to be happening and we can become frustrated and disheartened.

Some changes may well be felt very quickly, but those changes that required some pretty substantial re-wiring in our brain together with some major shifts in the reality we experience might take some time.

Watching for Signs

I am reminded of the story of the person standing under the snow covered tree and shaking it for all they were worth. As hard as they shook, no snow seemed to drop. What they couldn't see was actually how much movement there was at the top of the tree and how much snow was becoming loose. But seeing nothing happening, they became frustrated and shook the tree even harder. But then, without warning, the tree suddenly dumped the whole lot right on top of their head.

We will need to be watchful of any signs, coincidences and happen-chances which are probably good signs of the aforementioned mysterious ways. It is said there is no such thing as coincidence or luck and during our journey of discovery we may well find this out. This could involve someone coming into your life unexpectedly, or a sudden change in circumstances that opens up new possibilities or a sudden opportunity that appears out of nowhere that might even appear to have negative consequences in the short term.

These coincidences and opportunities will present themselves in response to the stream of positive energy you are putting out there. They may not look like opportunities at the time and you should therefore remain especially vigilant to recognise them and to take advantage.

Georgia: I strongly believe in the fact that like attracts like, and a positive outlook attracts positive outcomes and people. This is tried and tested in my personal life. When I am feeling positive and driven and determined, and step out of my own way I am always blown away by the people and situations that manifest.

Give it a chance

Once a gardener has planted his seeds in the well prepared ground and provided the weather does its bit, the seeds should grow into what is expected. The gardener does not usually stare at the ground and look at his watch, nor does he dig up the seeds from time to time to make sure they are growing. Instead, the gardener has faith that the right things have been done and therefore the right things will happen, eventually.

Michael Neil in his book, *You can have what you want*, says: *You should hold your dreams as you would a butterfly: Hard enough to keep it from escaping, but not so hard as to crush it in your grasp.*

In the same way, *provided* we continue to put our energy and actions out there, we should be confident of success. Indeed, the very nature of the intention process requires just that – it requires *Total Faith, Confidence and Expectation.*

What we must avoid is to worry our dreams to death, which will bring our ego back into play and prevent our *Authentic Energy* from changing our reality.

Ash: *I am a dreamer and fantasist, often imagining the life and end goal that I want. This however isn't always a good idea. Too much time focused on the end goal means that the present is often wished away or passed without too much care and attention. Relying on this end goal happening on its own accord is also dangerous, I know that my actions and decisions NOW are the things that are going to determine my path, and I try to focus on this.*

Challenging the Myth – Not an excuse to sit on your hands

This probably represents one of the biggest issues in the *whole 7-Step* process – how do you strongly visualise the result, but still allow the universe some leeway in making it happen? Not having detailed plans for every step of your goal and allowing the universe some wriggle room and latitude with its timescales is not the same as allowing yourselves to sit on our hands to wait for things to happen.

Keeping your goals and energy to yourself will not give the universe much to work with and you must therefore give it as much help as you can for it to help you. We therefore have to take *Action*, that puts our *WOW! Energy* into the external world, to create those opportunities that we then must follow-up enthusiastically and energetically.

If you feel that you are trying to swim against the current, this probably means that you are putting too much pressure on your intentions and not allowing your energy and the universe to deliver in their own way.

You are therefore trying to control everything or trying to force outcomes or worrying about all the details of achieving your goals. Given what we have said earlier about the nature of transformational change, this is likely to be counter-productive.

Our new *Beliefs and Expectations* which are now hard-wired are always at work and we should have faith that they will bear fruit. Again, this is not an excuse to sit on our hands but to remind ourselves not to become obsessive about our goals to the point where they are taking us away from being fully engaged in the here and now.

Rennie: I think I have fallen for the trap of thinking that affirmations and visualizations are sufficient on their own rather than realising that these techniques are more important in creating our internal energy that stimulates our action and behaviour. I now realise that attention and intention are important but they need to be followed up by action. This action then takes our energy and intention out in the world which I believe to be the mechanism for creating change to our situation. This led me to be wary of those books that claim we can make changes by just thinking about them. I think this is a good start but only the start.

Be careful what you wish for

Notwithstanding what we said above, it could be that you get exactly what you have asked for and exactly when you want it. You should therefore be very careful about your thoughts and your intentions as you might just order something unintentionally. This is a bit like accidentally twitching at the wrong time during an auction and accidentally buying that massive stuffed mammoth that you didn't really want.

This comes back to the essential issue of *Mindful Awareness* and of being in better control of our thoughts and emotions. We are creating thought energy and emotional energy all the time and it is always having an affect whether we can see it or not. This energy constantly radiates through our body controlling our body processes and constantly radiating through the rest of space affecting everything else.

Keeping the Faith

We have already spoken about how the fulfilment of our *WOWS* and *Life Goals* is not an exact science and our precise inputs may not be matched by precise outputs. The road ahead is likely to be full of false starts or dead-ends and it is therefore vital that all through this process we keep the faith in our *Authentic Self* and in our *WOW! Energy.*

What we believe we can do and what we expect to happen, together with our *WOW Energy-in-Motion* contains the transformational power that will ultimately make the right things happen.

We should also be careful of sharing our life goals too early as those around us might think they are doing us a favour by forcing us to *be realistic* and might therefore impose their own agenda and self-interests on us, even without realising it.

However, there are other people around us, with the right energy, who can offer invaluable help and support, which might even be essential for us to go forward. Such people might help us rather than discourage us.

Rennie: There were times when I felt overwhelmed by this book as it took over my entire life to the exclusion of everything else. The stamina, financial, emotional and intellectual challenge has been considerable and at times almost too difficult to handle.

But I have been driven on by my belief that what I am doing is the right thing and totally in line with my authentic self and life goals. This has always renewed my energy and determination to complete what I set out to do, no matter what. I have also been helped by those around me, particularly my wife and family who have recognised I am being authentic and doing what I am supposed to do and have therefore responded by encouraging me to keep going and by allowing me to focus on this project.

Enjoy the journey

What is the mechanism for getting there in the end? Our genes want to be expressed and will always be looking for an opportunity and therefore any change of environment, new situation or random thought might trigger them. This is why I have the belief that provided we are putting our authentic energy out there, we will get there in the end even if by a long and circuitous route.

We should remember throughout the *7-Steps* that our journey towards *Personal Fulfilment* is not just a means to an end but is also an end in itself. Even though we are being our *Authentic Self*, galvanised by our *WOW! Energy* and heading towards our *Life Purpose*, we still remain totally engaged in the present moment and in the ideal position to exploit this state of mind and to fully experience everything around us.

We should acknowledge and celebrate all of those coincidences, happen-chances or slices of luck that we will experience along the way, together with every small success that takes us further towards our goals. This will strengthen those positive emotions that are so important to our sense of well-being and will further confirm our *Belief and Expectation* that the right things are in fact happening.

Change the inner then the outer

Whatever we believe about the nature of reality and our influence upon it, we need to remember that the biggest changes need to be made within before we can expect to change anything else.

Therefore we must *first change our inner before we can change our outer*, as it is the combination of the changes we have made to what we believe, what we do and what we now expect to happen that will change the external reality we experience.

Not only is our *Authentic and WOW! Energy* responsible for influencing everything about us and for motivating us to achieve our life goals, but it will also be felt by everyone around us, who will find this energy infectious and attractive. This is probably the technology behind the *Law of Attraction*, which could be the result of our energy resonating with like-minded people or in creating beneficial opportunities and situations.

THE PARABLE OF THE PRODUCER AND THE MIXING DESK

There is a producer in a music recording studio, sitting behind a mixing desk and listening to a full orchestra playing a symphony. The orchestra started off as a small group of musicians around the time the producer was born with their own original and distinctive sound but later developed into a full-blown orchestra with a more extensive repertoire over the course of the producer's lifetime.

The producer listens to a playback of the tape and

although generally happy, decides to more fully exploit certain instruments whilst lessening the influence of others to create a different mix of sounds that in the producer's belief creates an even better experience.

The producer therefore plays around with all those sliding switches on the mixing desk to create the ideal symphony by emphasizing the lighter and more melodic strings and by lessening the impact of the louder and harsher brass section. Eventually the producer is delighted with the finished recording as it reflects the music the producer wants to create.

The producer plays the new symphony over and over again until it becomes second nature and burned deep within the producer's memory, but when brought to mind, never ceases to gladden and energize every element of the producer's being. The CD that is then released into the outside world has an amazing effect on everybody that hears it, with many people asking if live concerts are planned.

The Full Process

We can now summarise the whole process with the following diagram showing how our New Authentic Self was discovered and how it now influences every part of our lives:

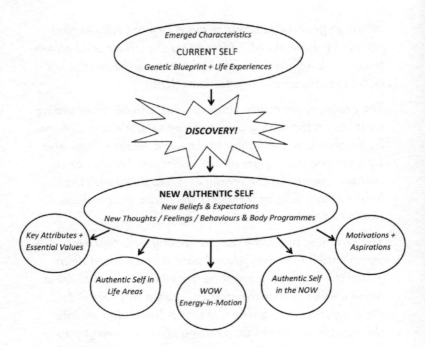

Nearly There

Any remaining Limiting Beliefs?

Throughout this book, we have been following a positive philosophy that looks to exploit our *Key Attributes and Essential Values* in all areas of our life and ultimately for these things to help us achieve our *Life Goals and Life Purpose.*

My initial belief, that follows the theory of the great *Carl Jung,* was that the *7 Steps* would effectively address many of our emotional or psychological issues we may have had.

It was hoped that many of the things we all suffer from such as a lack of confidence, anxiety, frustration or tension, would therefore melt away as we became more authentic and increasingly imposed this true self on the outside world.

My view was that rather than deal with the symptom (lack of confidence) it would be more effective to deal with what this lack of confidence prevented us from doing (being our authentic self). Therefore, as we began to feel and to be authentic, any lack of confidence might well have diminished to further strengthen our belief that this is how things can be from now on.

Learning to live with it

If we scratch the surface of even those seemingly well-adjusted of individuals, we will probably find they are also managing their own issues to varying levels of success. We may therefore come to realise that some our less positive characteristics and pre-dispositions will always be there and therefore to erase them completely is just not possible. But in the same way that we have sought to bring out and exploit our more positive attributes we can learn to live with our less positive traits and more negative pre-dispositions.

We might for example always be prone to anxiety or to a lack of confidence, but we can learn how to manage these issues towards the lower end of their set-range where they have a much reduced impact on our lives.

As Martin Seligman says in *What You Can Change and What You Can't: Negative emotions and negative personality traits have very strong biological limits and perhaps the best that science and practice can do is to encourage people to live in the best part of their set range of psychological symptoms. Therefore, an old fashioned virtue must be coupled to the various interventions and this is courage: the courage to understand your psychological problems and manage them so as to function well in spite of them.*

So the question is, has this positive philosophy worked? Have you learned to just get on with it, or do you still have some remaining issues you would like to address? (See the Exercises at the end of this step).

Compromises?

Our *Positive Philosophy* has been aimed to ensure that we became our authentic self and therefore I tried to discourage you from making any compromises before we had arrived at this point, particularly as it might have been previous compromises that had prevented you from being who you should be in the first place.

But now, from a position of *Authentic Strength*, we can afford to make compromises at this much later stage, knowing that any such compromise will not deflect us from our being who we are and might just help us win the support of important others who can help us towards our goals.

Therefore, do we need to *adapt* our behaviour, goals or plans to better accommodate other people's wishes?

Or have you found that your authentic and *WOW Energy* has been so infectious that the people you thought you would have to make compromises for have in fact stepped forward with their positive support? As with *Limiting Beliefs*, has the need for compromise simply melted away?

Further work?

When we took a look at our *Key Attributes* and *Essential Values*, you may have also identified some *Signature Weaknesses* if you like, i.e. those things that we are not particularly good at or the less positive aspects of our personality. If you took the online *VIA Character Strengths Questionnaire*, I asked you to put these so-called weaknesses to one side and to concentrate on the more positive aspects of your personality.

As with *Limiting Beliefs* and compromises, there may now be some things you might like to address as they might actually be getting in the way of you achieving what you want to achieve?

Perhaps you might also want to re-visit my questionnaire to see what progress you have made or whether there are some remaining issues to be addressed on your path to *Self-Awareness and Personal Fulfilment* which will further strengthen your new *Authentic Thoughts, Beliefs and Behaviour*.

A Lifelong Practice

We have made enormous progress in our *Self-Awareness and Personal Fulfilment*, but of course, this process never really ends. Our aspirations change as does our situation and therefore we should continue to practice many of the things we have become familiar with. Certainly *Mindfulness* and those elements in *Well-Being* and the continuous focus on our *Authenticity, WOWS! Goals and Life Purpose* should perhaps become a lifelong practice?

The Big Finish...

Personal Fulfilment is as much about the journey as it is about the destination. Being filled with *Authentic WOW! Energy* gives our life excitement and meaning. We are being the fullest expression of our authentic self. What can be more exciting and meaningful than that? Our energy is therefore coursing through our veins and lighting up every part of our being in the fulfilment of our *Life Purpose*.

This is surely the highest state of being and in the final analysis, whatever happens in the external world is probably less important than how we now feel inside.

We might never exactly achieve those *Life Goals* that were responsible for creating our *WOW! Energy* in the first place but does this really matter as this energy will surely create other opportunities and results that are equally exciting and fulfilling.

In the *Introduction,* I said that this book supported the more rational and humanistic view of life that assumes our essential self comes from within rather than from without, but in the final analysis, does it really matter where we are coming from, as life is arguably all about being who we are to the best of our ability and then about helping others to do the same. Whether this is for the glory of a God or to celebrate our own humanity is surely immaterial?

We are finally being who we should always have been and doing what we should always have been doing and whatever happens in the future will be the authentic result of this energy galvanising our every moment and resonating with the outside world – an irresistible force meeting a moveable object.

Review Questions

The objective of these review questions is not to test your understanding but to allow you to reflect on some of the issues raised in this step and also to help you prepare for the exercises that follow.

1. *Are you trying too hard or fretting over specific outcomes?*

2. *Are you taking time to smell the roses along the way?*

3. *Are you putting enough authentic or WOW energy out there?*

4. *Are you expecting the best to happen?*

5. *Are you giving the universe some wriggle room but seizing opportunities when they arise?*

Exercises

As was said in the main introduction, you certainly do not have to complete all the exercises but just try the ones that appeal to you.

Exercise 1 - Looking for signs / Seizing opportunities

1. *What signs and opportunities have already appeared as if by magic?*

2. *What opportunities have recently appeared cunningly disguised as problems?*

3. *In which areas of life will you pay particular attention to from now on?*

Exercise 2 – Enjoy the journey / Celebrating Success

At various points during the day just pause and recount the good things that have happened.

Exercise 3 – Signature Weaknesses

If you took the online VIA Character Strengths questionnaire, you might remember that I asked you to keep a note of those attributes where you scored the lowest.

1.   *What were your weaknesses?*

2.   *How might they be an obstacle to your Self Fulfilment?*

3.   *What are you going to do about them?*

Exercise 4 – Limiting Beliefs / Fears

Similarly, as part of the strategy of the 7-Steps, I asked at the start of this process for to mainly concentrate on your strengths rather than on your weaknesses, but now is the time to revisit this question to ask yourself whether any issues still remain that need addressing as we are now in a much better place to confront any residual limiting beliefs or fears

1.   *Choose the Limiting Belief or fear you want to change (e.g. Low Confidence)*

2.   *Now generate your New Positive Self-Image and add any new attribute you want to include in this image (such as Confidence)*

3.   *Pick an area of your life where you would like to be this New Confident You (perhaps where you have previously had a confidence problem) and visualize this scenario with you being confident with as much*

emotion as you can muster and watch what you can achieve

4. When appropriate take those confident actions in that area of life for real and feel your confidence grow further in line with your success

5. As your confidence grows, set yourself further goals for what your confidence can now achieve and take those further actions as your new confident self

6. Keep reminding yourself of your New Confident Image and of your Visualization of you being Confident in the situation you want

This Personal Image of this new confident you can also be used to go backwards in time to re-write your life experiences in a more positive way.

Exercise 5 – Unpleasant Memories

This is to learn how to change an unpleasant memory.

1. Think of an everyday problem and pick a real event from your past which demonstrates the problem. Watch a movie of the situation in question and be aware how you are feeling

2. Select some theme music that is inappropriate to the feelings you generated such as circus music for example

3. Play your music in your head as you watch your old movie again that illustrated your issue and either run it faster or backwards so that it looks silly and laugh at it.

4. When you play your movie and again, do you now automatically hear the music and see the film going

fast or backwards and laugh? Keep repeating the silly music and video until this happens

Exercise 6 – Compromises?

You will hopefully remember that I discouraged you from making compromises too early, before you had found the confidence to be your authentic self. Well, as you are now in a position of strength you are in a better position to make compromises, which are of course a two-way thing.

1. *Is there anyone you need to bring along with you?*

2. *Is there anyone who you would like to make a compromise for?*

3. *Is there something you could give as a compromise to get something important back in return?*

4. *Would a personal compromise from you be helpful to anyone in some way?*

But remembering that any compromise should not materially deflect you from being who you are and from doing what you need to do.

Exercise 7 – Revisit Questionnaire

Perhaps it is now time to revisit the questionnaire to see what progress you have made and where you might want to target your next development?

Hopefully you will find that you have addressed a number of issues you identified at the start and this knowledge of your progress should inspire you to continue on your (never ending) journey of self-awareness and personal fulfilment.

GRATITUDE

7 Steps to Self-Awareness & Personal Fulfilment

GRATITUDE *Now Give Back*	
FULFILMENT *Make it Happen*	
EXPRESSION *Release your WOW*	Personal Fulfilment ↑
WELL-BEING *Now Flourish!*	
AUTHENTICITY *Become the Real You*	
AWARENESS *Control your Mind*	Self-Awareness ↑
INSIGHT *What you should know*	

Introduction

This is the final step in the book and a relatively short one as we have done most of the work we need to do. However, up until now, most of this work has been focussed on ourselves so that we can fully exploit our unique attributes and make our own unique contribution. We should therefore be feeling much more self-aware with a much greater sense of self-fulfilment.

A major aspect of this personal fulfilment is to be grateful for who we are and to give thanks for our opportunities and gifts, but it is equally important to recognise the unique contribution that everyone can make and to use our knowledge, insights and abilities to help others make this contribution and to give back.

Being Grateful

Making the most of who we are

Perhaps the best way to show gratitude is to fully exploit our unique abilities to maximum effect and in so doing, we will fully experience our life to the full. We could argue that we owe this to our ancestors who survived against all the odds to pass their genes on to the next generation and finally to us. We could also argue that it is in the interests of the human race as a whole that we become the best we can be to push our species on to the next phase in its development, whatever that is.

Grateful for what we have

We have already discussed this in *Well-Being*, but it's worth repeating that a major part of gratitude is to be grateful for what we already have in our lives. In particular, we should feel grateful for our positive and uplifting memories and experiences and for our relationships, particularly with our family and close friends. Research has shown that such things are the true source of long-term happiness and sound physical and emotional health, rather than the accumulation of money or status.

Additionally, as our knowledge of how the brain works tells us we are more inclined to emphasise and remember our negative experiences, perhaps we should pay more attention and remember our positive experiences in the course of our daily lives in order to counter our negative tendencies. This is particularly important last thing at night and first thing in the morning when our relaxed mind is particularly suggestible and more likely to take on board what we are thinking to set our mood.

As Hans Selye (someone who researched into the causes of stress) once said, *Imitate the sundials ways; count only the pleasant days.*

Grateful for what we have achieved

A further part of this gratitude is to remind ourselves about what we have already achieved.

Our accomplishments and successes and those things we are most proud of.

Our success in dealing with any challenges or set-backs

Everything we have learned and for all the valuable experience we have accumulated over our lifetime.

We might also want to be grateful for the opportunity the 7-Steps has provided to reflect on who we really are and to identify our true *Authentic Self*. This has given us the chance to wipe the slate clean and to start-over with a renewed sense of energy, confidence and belief, to create an environment that better reflects our legitimate attributes, values, motivations and aspirations.

Giving Back

The Bigger Picture

In *Insight*, we talked about the origins of the universe and how we all sprang from the same source and from the same stuff and understood from our physicist friends that *once connected, always connected.* If this wasn't enough, we have also learned we are all immersed in the same energy field that produces the very matter from which we are all made. All of which suggests we are entangled in weird and wonderful ways that we might never fully understand.

There are therefore those who believe our individual thoughts, feelings and actions have a much wider influence on the world around us and on our collective experience than we have traditionally thought. Perhaps this is the true source of *karma* and also the basis for those traditional sayings:

You must give in order to receive.

As you sow, so will you reap.

Even if we don't feel any responsibility for the well-being of anyone else, the evidence suggests that it's in our own self-interest to be more empathetic towards others as these feelings have a beneficial effect on our own well-being.

Helping others find their own way

As mentioned in the introduction, given that we have arrived at this advanced stage in our journey towards *Self-Awareness and Personal Fulfilment,* perhaps it is now time to use our unique abilities to help others do the same? In this way, *The 7-Steps* are not just a selfish doctrine, only concerned with our own ultimate fulfilment, but they also embrace the wider good.

Giving is often more satisfying than receiving and therefore we should all benefit from giving our time and energies to help others achieve their life purpose and to make their fullest contribution. In a very real sense to help others is to help ourselves. So the question is, how could you use your *Key Attributes* and *Essential Values* to help others?

Georgia: I absolutely believe in helping others and have in the past been known to do so at the detriment of my own health or well-being. I am more balanced now (I believe), but absolutely get so very much out of making someone else smile. It is a huge driver for me, and one that I get so much from. Life for me, is about making other people happy and helping to make a difference and in doing so it feeds my soul. And what seems to amaze some people is that the more you do it the better you feel, and the more you get back but it is so very true. Smiling is infectious!

Kindness

Spontaneous Acts

Do not underestimate the impact that a *Spontaneous Act of Kindness* can have on a complete stranger. Just imagine if it was a personal objective of everyone to offer acts of kindness as a matter of course. Perhaps we should have a *Spontaneous Act of Kindness Day?* In any event, couldn't we all seek out creative opportunities to be kind to others, perhaps by even setting ourselves a daily target?

Just as with *Giving Back*, kindness to others works for the giver as well as for the receiver. If we can make someone's day with a spontaneous act of kindness, however small, we can experience an inner glow that can last all day or even longer and it is also more likely that people will be kind to us in return – like attracting like.

Susie: I know from experience the incredible feeling to be gained from helping others – I think sometimes I get so bogged down in what I am doing that I don't look up and see opportunity to help others enough. This is something I probably had never considered until now...

The Positive Impact of Empathy

A major part of giving back and kindness is the ability to demonstrate compassion and empathy for others. For some of us, this is an essential part of our make-up and such things come naturally, whereas for others, these feelings are not as forthcoming, particularly if we are struggling with some of our own issues.

There is evidence that compassion and empathy have a positive effect on our brain and makes us more calm and balanced, which is again another example of what is good for others is also good for ourselves.

A Creed?

My friend Joe suggested I finish the book with a strong conclusion that summarises the key messages. I hope these words do the job as they represent my own personal creed:

Find out what you love doing and just do it
Put your heart and soul into this one thing
Don't listen to anyone who tells you different
Look for the joy in all things
Help others find their own way

Review Questions

The objective of these review questions is not to test your understanding but to allow you to reflect on some of the issues raised in this step and also to help you prepare for the exercises that follow.

1. *Do you feel grateful for who you are and for your unique gifts?*

2. *Are you paying particular attention to all your positive experiences?*

3. *Are you extracting joy from even the simplest of things?*

4. *How might you us your Key Attributes and Essential Values to give back?*

5. *Are you looking for opportunities to perform spontaneous acts of kindness?*

Exercises

As was said in the main introduction, you certainly do not have to complete all the exercises but just try the ones that appeal to you.

BEING GRATEFUL

Exercise 1 - Creating a Positive Daily Routine

Before Sleep - Remembering the Positives

We want to go to sleep with our mind full of positive thoughts so that our subconscious is primed to work its magic when we are asleep.

So, just before you go to sleep at night do the following:

1. *Take a few deep breaths and then visualize your image*

of your Authentic Self that contains your Key Attributes and Essential Values

2. *Give thanks for who you are, the relationships you have, what you have achieved and what you are doing with your life*

3. *Remember all the positive things you have done and that happened in your day and really flood your mind with all the sensations these memories create*

4. *(Optional) Ask your subconscious to work overnight to provide an answer to an issue or a problem you have (Don't be concerned about overloading your subconscious as it easily has enough processing power to deal with all this)*

On Waking - Looking forward with expectation

1. *Take a few deep breaths and then visualize your image of your Authentic Self that contains your Key Attributes and Essential Values*

2. *Really luxuriate in who you are and your uniqueness*

3. *(Optional) Now feel your WOWS that represent your Life Goals in pursuit of your Life Purpose*

4. *Do some mindful stretches and really pay attention to what your body is doing and feeling*

5. *Catch yourself being aware throughout the day and practice mindfulness even during the simplest of tasks*

Exercise 2 - The Gratitude Visit / Message

Feelings of gratitude and thanks have a very positive impact by releasing all manner of positive chemicals in our brain and then around our body, so as well as making others feel good, gratitude works powerfully on ourselves.

So, give thanks to someone either personally or via any kind of message and tell them how you feel:

- *Someone who is important to you*

- *Someone whose help was very important at a particular time in your life*

- *Someone you admire or inspired you to do something*

- *Someone who brings you happiness and joy*

Exercise 3 - Gratitude Meditation

A good way to support feelings of gratitude kindness is via a compassion meditation.

1. *First take some deep breaths and focus on an object for a while in the usual way, whether it's your breath or something visual or anything at all really as meditation is about control and focus of awareness, nothing else.*

2. *So when you are fully relaxed, perhaps with your eyes closed, you can begin to have positive thoughts and feelings of happiness and gratitude for everything in your life.*

3. *Feel this happiness and gratitude taking over your thoughts and feelings. Luxuriate in them for as long as you want and let them fully take you over.*

GIVING BACK

Exercise 4 - Using our Key Attributes & Essential Values to help others

So far we have focused on using our Key Attributes and

Essential Values for our own benefit but now we can look to use them specifically for the benefit of others, although of course this might already be part of your life purpose.

So, how do you think you could use your authentic self and authentic energy to help others?

KINDNESS

Exercise 5 – *Spontaneous acts of kindness*

This is a very powerful exercise and really brightens your own day as well as perhaps making the day special for someone else. I set myself a target of one spontaneous act of kindness per day, but this is a tough target and I need to be vigilant and imaginative to meet it!

Look for opportunities to help others, even strangers, with small but significant acts of kindness:

Helping someone lift heavy bags or a pushchair up a flight of stairs

Giving that 5p to the next person in the coffee shop who doesn't quite have the right change

Buying that carton of milk for the person queuing to pay just for this one thing

Exercise 6 – *Compassion Meditation*

A good way to support kindness is via a compassion meditation.

1. *First take some deep breaths and focus on an object for a while in the usual way.*

2. *When you are fully relaxed, perhaps with your eyes closed, you can begin to have kind and positive*

thoughts and feelings about someone who you are close to. Feel the compassion and empathy and love taking over your thoughts and feelings. Luxuriate in these thoughts and feelings for as long as you want and let them fully take you over.

3. You can then start to move these thoughts and feelings around to take in other people you might know, even those you don't like or have had issues with. Wrap these people in your compassionate thoughts and feelings too.

Appendix 1

Questionnaire

Release your WOW!

7 Steps to Self-awareness & Personal Fulfilment

This questionnaire is designed to help readers identify their current levels of Self-Awareness and Personal Fulfilment in each of the 7-Steps.

Please read through each section and consider your response to the questions, entering your score in the relevant box that best approximates how you feel about each question. Then at the end of each section, summarise what you think you have learned about yourself.

Finally, on the last page, calculate your total score and summarise what you think it all means for you and identify those areas where you might find any further guidance useful.

Release your WOW!

7 Steps to Self-awareness & Personal Fulfilment

Step 7	GRATITUDE
Step 6	FULFILMENT
Step 5	EXPRESSION
Step 4	WELL-BEING
Step 3	AUTHENTICITY
Step 2	AWARENESS
Step 1	INSIGHT

Step 1 INSIGHT – What you should know

1.1   I know my genetic blueprint is only half of the story of who I am and I know where the other half comes from

Very untrue	Untrue	Some-what untrue	Neither True or Untrue	Some-what true	True	Very true
-3	-2	-1	0	+1	+2	+3

1.2   I understand how my mind transmits my intentions to the rest of my brain and throughout my body

Very untrue	Untrue	Some-what untrue	Neither True or Untrue	Some-what true	True	Very true
-3	-2	-1	0	+1	+2	+3

1.3   I understand how brain plasticity and epigenetics provides the opportunity to re-configure my brain to change how I think, feel and behave

Very untrue	Untrue	Some-what untrue	Neither True or Untrue	Some-what true	True	Very true
-3	-2	-1	0	+1	+2	+3

Step 2 AWARENESS – Control your Mind

2.1   My inner calm comes from being grounded in the present moment and from my ability to "just be"

Very untrue	Untrue	Some-what untrue	Neither True or Untrue	Some-what true	True	Very true
-3	-2	-1	0	+1	+2	+3

2.2 In order to focus my attention, I practice mindfulness, even during the simplest of tasks

Very untrue	Untrue	Some-what untrue	Neither True or Untrue	Some-what true	True	Very true
-3	-2	-1	0	+1	+2	+3

2.3 I am able to take an observer perspective to reflect on my own thoughts, feelings and current situation

Very untrue	Untrue	Some-what untrue	Neither True or Untrue	Some-what true	True	Very true
-3	-2	-1	0	+1	+2	+3

Step 3 AUTHENTICITY – Become the real you

3.1 I practice acceptance and self-forgiveness as an essential step for moving forward

Very untrue	Untrue	Some-what untrue	Neither True or Untrue	Some-what true	True	Very true
-3	-2	-1	0	+1	+2	+3

3.2 I have a good insight into my particular Key Attributes & Essential Values, together with the other positive aspects of my personality

Very untrue	Untrue	Some-what untrue	Neither True or Untrue	Some-what true	True	Very true
-3	-2	-1	0	+1	+2	+3

3.3 I demonstrate all the confidence that comes from knowing who I am and this Authentic Self fully engages in every moment

Very untrue	Untrue	Some-what untrue	Neither True or Untrue	Some-what true	True	Very true
-3	-2	-1	0	+1	+2	+3

Step 4 WELL-BEING - Now Flourish!

4:1 I have special places and special memories where I can go in my mind to transform my mood

Very untrue	Untrue	Some-what untrue	Neither True or Untrue	Some-what true	True	Very true
-3	-2	-1	0	+1	+2	+3

4.2 I am exploiting my key attributes and essential values in all areas of life and celebrate my successes and accomplishments

Very untrue	Untrue	Some-what untrue	Neither True or Untrue	Some-what true	True	Very true
-3	-2	-1	0	+1	+2	+3

4.3 Although I sometimes experience disappointments, I am able to bounce back fairly quickly to feel positive again

Very untrue	Untrue	Some-what untrue	Neither True or Untrue	Some-what true	True	Very true
-3	-2	-1	0	+1	+2	+3

Step 5 EXPRESSION - Release your WOW!

5.1   I am very clear what my ideal life or future looks like and this gives me a WOW just thinking about it

Very untrue	Untrue	Some-what untrue	Neither True or Untrue	Some-what true	True	Very true
-3	-2	-1	0	+1	+2	+3

5:2   Visualizing my WOWS give me the energy to pursue my Life Goals and Life Purpose

Very untrue	Untrue	Some-what untrue	Neither True or Untrue	Some-what true	True	Very true
-3	-2	-1	0	+1	+2	+3

5:3   My WOW energy seems to attract like-minded people and opportunities towards me

Very untrue	Untrue	Some-what untrue	Neither True or Untrue	Some-what true	True	Very true
-3	-2	-1	0	+1	+2	+3

Step 6 FULFILMENT - Make it happen

6:1   Although I often visualize my WOWS & my life's goals, I remain grounded in the present moment where everything happens

Very untrue	Untrue	Some-what untrue	Neither True or Untrue	Some-what true	True	Very true
-3	-2	-1	0	+1	+2	+3

6:2 My life goals are like a star in the sky that keeps me moving in the right direction and focused on doing the right things

Very untrue	Untrue	Some-what untrue	Neither True or Untrue	Some-what true	True	Very true
-3	-2	-1	0	+1	+2	+3

6:3 I am quick to exploit those situations and opportunities that appear as if by magic to move me towards my goals

Very untrue	Untrue	Some-what untrue	Neither True or Untrue	Some-what true	True	Very true
-3	-2	-1	0	+1	+2	+3

Step 7 GRATITUDE – Help others along the way

7:1 I often give thanks for my life; for its gifts and opportunities

Very untrue	Untrue	Some-what untrue	Neither True or Untrue	Some-what true	True	Very true
-3	-2	-1	0	+1	+2	+3

7.2 I am now exploiting the positive aspects of who I am to help others find their own way and to make their own unique contribution

Very untrue	Untrue	Some-what untrue	Neither True or Untrue	Some-what true	True	Very true
-3	-2	-1	0	+1	+2	+3

7.3 I practice spontaneous acts of kindness, often to complete strangers which also contributes to my own well-being

Very untrue	Untrue	Some-what untrue	Neither True or Untrue	Some-what true	True	Very true
-3	-2	-1	0	+1	+2	+3

Scores:

STEP	MINIMUM SCORE	MAXIMUM SCORE	YOUR SCORE
Step 1 INSIGHT	-9	+9	
Step 2 AWARENESS	-9	+9	
Step 3 AUTHENTICITY	-9	+9	
Step 4 WELL-BEING	-9	+9	
Step 5 EXPRESSION	-9	+9	
Step 6 FULFILMENT	-9	+9	
Step 7 GRATITUDE	-9	+9	
TOTAL	-63	+63	

Interpretation:

The score for each statement has a range of -9 to +9 and therefore a score of 0 means that the statement is neither untrue nor true of you.

The more negative the score, the more untrue this statement is of you, whereas the more positive the score, the more true this statement is of you.

Ideally, we are looking to develop towards the positive end of the scale for each statement and for each step and therefore your scores will help you identify your current situation and those areas you might like to address to achieve a greater sense of *Self-Awareness* and *Personal Fulfilment*.

Appendix 2

What we can change

I thought it might be useful at this point to make a list of everything we can change to achieve Self-Awareness and Personal Fulfilment.

We can:

1. *Accept who we are but discover our true authentic self*

2. *Exploit our full potential*

3. *Trigger dormant potentials or operate at the higher end of our genetic set-range*

4. *Ameliorate negative pre-dispositions / emphasize positive pre-dispositions*

5. *Re-set our Autopilots (Thoughts, Feelings, Behaviour, Bodily Processes)*

6. *Re-configure our brain by creating new wiring and connections*

7. *Change our Belief & Expectations filter*

8. *Re-frame past experiences to make them more positive*

9. *Create a storehouse of positive memories and emotion*

10. *Become more mindful and aware*

11. *Focus on the more positive aspects of life to overrule our negative bias*

12. *Extract more joy from our normal experiences*

13. *Show more gratitude and be kinder to others*

14. *Become more satisfied, content and happy*

15. *Become more optimistic about the future*

16. *More fully engage and experience the present moment*

17. *Take better control of our feelings (associate into positive feelings / Dis-associate from negative feelings)*

18. *Find meaning and purpose*

19. *Bring peace and tranquillity to our mind*

20. *Become more reflective and evaluate our situation*

21. *Become happier and more Authentic in our current areas of life*

22. *Create more positive relationships and a more positive personal infrastructure*

23. *Get better at anything through effort and practice*

24. *Learn new skills and even learn by just watching others*

25. *Galvanize ourselves with Authentic & WOW! energy*

26. *Put this energy out into the world to make things happen*

27. *Pursue our Life Goals & WOWS!*

28. *Fulfil our Life Purpose*

29. *Give to others*

30. *Challenge our autopilot behaviours by trying new things*

31. *Celebrate successes*

Booklist

The following is a list of the books that provided the references found in my book, together with some other titles that I found useful during the book's research and development phase.

Neuroscience

Rewire Your Brain – John B Arden

Change Your Brain Change Your Life – Daniel G Amen

The Plastic Mind – Sharon Begley

Incognito – David Eagleman

The Emotional Life of your Brain – Richard Davidson

The Brain, a Very Short Introduction – Michael O'Shea

The Tell-Tale Brain – VS Ramachandran

A mind of its own – Cordelia Fine

Mindfulness & Epigenetics

Mindfulness – Mark Williams & Danny Penman

Nature v Nurture – Matt Ridley

The Epigenetics Revolution – Nessa Carey

The Biology of Belief – Bruce Lipton

The Genie Within Your Genes – Dawson Church

Positive Psychology

Authentic Happiness – Martin Seligman

What You Can Change and What You Can't – Martin Seligman

Flourish – Martin Seligman

Flow – Mihaly Csikszentmihalyi

Positive Psychology – Miriam Akhtar

Mindset – Carol S Dwek

Other

Quantum – Jim Al-Khalili

The Power of Your Subconscious Mind – Joseph Murphy

The Monk Who Sold His Ferrari – Robin Sharma

Feel The Fear & Do It Anyway – Susan Jeffers

NLP – Steve Andreas & Charles Faulkner

It's the Thought That Counts – David R Hamilton

You Can Have What You Want – Michael Neill

Why Evolution Is True – Jerry A Coyne

Synchrodestiny – Deepak Chopra

The Seven Spiritual Laws of Success – Deepak Chopra

Conversations with God – Donald Walsch

A New Earth – Eckhart Tolle

The Power of Now – Eckhart Tolle

INDEX

RENNIE GOULD

Website & Blog

For further information and additional resources, please go to:

www.renniegould.com

Release Your WOW! Workshops

For individual and group workshops, please go to:

www.releaseyourwow.com

Rennie Gould

Rennie Gould is a world renowned consultant, lecturer and writer who has worked with thousands of people around the world to help them achieve their personal and organisational goals. He usually describes himself as a semi-academic, with one foot in the world of academic theory and the other in the world of practical implementation, which is possibly the ideal background for the task he has taken on with this book.

Using his considerable gifts of investigation and communication, Rennie shares his unique 7-Step process for readers to make their own journey of Self-awareness and Personal Fulfilment and in so doing, he aptly demonstrates his own Life Purpose to Explain, Entertain and Inspire!

Urbane Publications is dedicated to
developing new author voices, and publishing
fiction and non-fiction that challenges, thrills and
fascinates.
From page-turning novels to innovative
reference books, our goal is to publish what
YOU want to read.
Find out more at
urbanepublications.com